HOMEBUILDING & RENOVATING MAGAZINE

BOOK OF

C000145148

GREAT ★ VALUE HOMES

25 INSPIRATIONAL HOMES
FROM £40,000-£241,000

192 PAGES ★ 225 COLOUR PHOTOS ★ 51 COLOUR ILLUSTRATIONS

an **ovolo** book

Ovolo Publishing Ltd
1 The Granary, Brook Farm,
Ellington, Huntingdon,
Cambridgeshire
PE28 0AE

This edition © 2007 Ovolo Publishing Ltd, 1 The Granary, Brook Farm, Ellington, Cambridgeshire PE28 0AE. Original text and illustrations © 2003-2007 Ascent Publishing Ltd, St Giles House, 50 Poland Street, London W1F 7AX

ISBN: 978 1 905959 02 0

All of the material in this book has previously appeared in Homebuilding & Renovating magazine - Britain's best selling monthly for selfbuilders and renovators (www.homebuilding.co.uk).

Book Design: Gill Lockhart
Publisher: Mark Neeter

This edition first published in the UK by Ovolo Publishing Ltd, October 2007
Printed in China

For more information on books about property and home interest please:
visit: www.buildingbooksdirect.com
email: info@ovolopublishing.co.uk
or call: 01480 891595 (24 hours)

CONTENTS

154 ↑ 14 ↑
◄174 132►

GREAT ★ VALUE HOMES

FOREWORD

EACH AND EVERY house in this book is a minor miracle, each one the triumph of imagination over budget and each firm evidence – if any is needed – that selfbuild works! In an age of government initiatives to build sustainable homes and deliver a better and more affordable built environment, the country's selfbuilders are leading the way.

Each of the houses in this book is individual as well as being delivered on a tight budget. Each house belongs in its respective setting and it is the fantastic variety that makes this collection of great value homes so inspirational.

These are not developer houses thrown up without care or attention to detail. These are quality buildings which reflect the thought and effort that has gone into their design and construction. Built to meet the specific needs of their owners.

These houses have been built in spite of our draconian planning laws which favour huge new developer-built settlements (often on greenfield sites). To allow limited, small-scale developments outside existing village boundaries would help to ease the pressure for new homes, would stop our villages from stagnating and would allow the genuinely innovative urges of selbuilders to take root across the whole breadth of this land.

However there are building plots out there if you know where to look – and each month in *Homebuilding & Renovating* magazine we help you. From a selection of land for sale to our regular Plotfinder Challenge feature we demonstrate just what can be found – if you know where to look.

This book is a great place to start looking for ideas. These homes may be 'budget' but they show that great things can be achieved with imagination, good design and careful management and there are many ways to build - from softwood timber frame, to oak frame or brick and block construction methods.

The inspirational stories on these pages demonstrate how you can achieve the same results. To help further we've included the details of architects, builders, contractors and suppliers involved in every one of the 25 houses.

With the inspiration and advice in this book, and your drive and determination, great things are not just possible, they're inevitable!

"WITH THE INSPIRATION AND ADVICE IN THIS BOOK, AND YOUR DRIVE AND DETERMINATION, GREAT THINGS ARE NOT JUST POSSIBLE, THEY'RE INEVITABLE."

Michael Holmes, Editor-in-Chief, Homebuilding & Renovating magazine

WHAT CAN YOU BUILD FOR UNDER £199,000?

**We present four fine examples
of the art of budget homebuilding.**

HIGH DESIGN

Michael and Elaine Yates' new home in Flintshire is of standard blockwork construction but its design is anything but ordinary. The house is totally site specific, with a south-facing deck and plenty of glass to make the most of the spectacular views over the Welsh countryside. It's the interior of the house, however, which belies the modest £190,000 build cost. Architect Michael has managed to create some interesting double-height spaces and a high-design contemporary feel – unusual for self-builders working to a relatively small budget.

Michael and Elaine Yates' house uses double height spaces for a contemporary feel.

**Build cost:
£190,000
House size: 224m²
Cost/m²: £848**

The whole family pitched in on this self-build and it's now worth over £400,000.

"DIY SAVED US A FORTUNE!"

When Andrew and Karen Gould relocated to Cornwall, they initially looked round for houses to buy to accommodate them and a granny annexe for Karen's mother – but nothing appealed and they hit upon self-build as the best way of getting the accommodation they needed. Working to a modest budget, Andrew planned out a detailed breakdown of costs on the timber frame project, but the project got off to a terrible start with the wrong choice of builder – and, some three months into the build, they found themselves deciding to take over the project. "We project managed, budgeted, purchased all materials, financially controlled and carried out most of the physical work ourselves," says Andrew. Apart from employing a new builder to make good some previous ➤

9

work, the Goulds really did take on much of the work themselves, which included: erection of the timber frame to first floor level; all plumbing and heating; all electrics (the work was completed prior to the new building regulations); finishing all internal rooms including dry-lining; laying floors and insulation; fitting all second fix materials; fitting all bathrooms and the kitchen, and all finishings.

Once the build got under way, Andrew and Karen decided to make the most of the attic space they were creating and turn it into an informal sitting/games room. As the project went on they also decided to upgrade the planned sanitaryware and fittings.

The project ended up taking two years to complete, with a build cost of £104,000 — all the more remarkable considering the house features five bedrooms over 325m². With a modest land cost, the Goulds have enjoyed a massive financial dividend on all their hard work, with the house valued at around £400,000.

Build cost: £104,000
House size: 325m²
Cost/m²: £320

Chris and Lucrecia's 100m² timber frame home is a perfect retreat – and took just seven months to build.

SIMPLE STYLE

Chris Mortimer and Lucrecia Luque's contemporary-style, open-plan home has all the design elements and quality of a high-end, high-budget project – but the home, on Skye, cost them just £66,000 to build. Keen to relocate from Brighton and enjoy a lifestyle in the great

outdoors, Chris and Lucrecia found a plot advertised on the internet and an article on the work of architects Dualchas, who create contemporary interpretations of the traditional Scottish crofter's cottage. Chris and Lucrecia's 100m² timber frame home is a perfect retreat – and took just seven months to build, featuring high-quality fittings, oak flooring and a range of clever design touches to separate out the spaces in the open plan space. The work was carried out by a main contractor, although Dualchas now operates a kit home company called Hebridean Homes (www.hebrideanhomes.com).

Build cost: £66,000
House size: 100m²
Cost/m²: £660

Chris and Lucrecia created a contemporary interpretation of a Scottish croft.

PRIORITY SPENDING

Robert Emmerson and Beverley Neilson's initial plan to renovate a charming old cottage in the beautiful Worcestershire countryside didn't turn out exactly as they had intended. Having bought the cottage, Robert and Beverley, who is the managing director of Fired Earth Interiors (www. firedearth.com), decided that having Beverley's parents close by would be an excellent idea and so moved them into the cottage and decided to

Robert and Beverley decided to upgrade cheaper items they installed in the future.

"TO KEEP WITHIN BUDGET WE DECIDED TO USE MORE COST-EFFECTIVE MATERIALS FOR SOME OF THE LESS-OBTRUSIVE FITTINGS, SUCH AS THE GUTTERING AND THE INTERNAL DOORS."

self-build in its garden.

In addition to Beverley's expertise in interiors, Robert has a wealth of experience having worked for a commercial housing developer – and working to a relatively modest budget, this proved essential. However, with hindsight, it is the areas where they tried to save money that irritate Robert the most. "To keep within budget we decided to use more cost-effective materials for some of the less-obtrusive fittings, such as the guttering and the internal doors, which we felt could be changed later should budgets permit. In an ideal world, we would have liked to have spent more on a better finish… and I would also like to incorporate bigger baths in the two bathrooms in the future."

Despite setbacks, such as having to spend £13,500 on foundations, a keen eye for a bargain and ensuring that three quotes were obtained for each job ensured that the project came in at £137,000. ■

Build cost: £137,000
House size: 200m²
Cost/m²: £685

Robert and Beverly decided to self-build in the grounds of their cottage

20 BUILDING BLOCKS OF A BUDGET SELF-BUILD

Ten-time self-builder David Snell reveals the best ways to ensure that you build a new home for under £199,000.

SET OUT YOUR BUDGET

1 Spend some time setting out your budget. Initially you may have to work on the basis of a cost per square metre, gleaned from case studies and the Build Cost Table in each month's edition of H&R. But once you start to get plans drawn, cost them out and relate them to your overall budget. Learn about labour costs and make use of companies that can quantify and cost your plans. This is an ongoing process and you may have to trim your ideas in order to keep to the original budget. Never lose sight of the fact that whatever you build must be capable of being built to your budget.

BUY THE RIGHT PLOT

The land is always going to form the biggest proportion of the costs of your self-build project. Most plots on the open market have a fixed price set by the estate agents involved and if you did try to haggle over the price, you'd probably lose it. On the other hand, plots that you have a hand in shaping can represent a considerable saving. If you identify a possible plot and tie things up with the owner so that you can buy it if you get planning permission, then you might expect to get the land at a discount.

"CO-ORDINATE THE SERVICES SO THAT ELECTRIC AND GAS SUPPLIERS CAN USE THE SAME TRENCH."

CHOOSE THE DESIGN WITH CARE

3 **Although there are other influences, it is always going to be the design that determines the costs of your project. Simple shapes will always be easier and cheaper to build than complex shapes, but that doesn't mean you have to compromise on good design. Many of the classic architectural forms – Georgian being one – rely on simplicity. Make sure that your designer is aware of costs and the cost implications of all design choices. Seek to maximise the usable volume of your home by occupying or planning to occupy the roof space. Avoid too many dormer windows and, instead, opt for rooflights.**

THINK ABOUT SPOIL

4 In any building project there are always vast amounts of spoil. At the beginning of the job, with materials coming in and the whole site churned up, the usual choice is to get rid of the spoil. But this is expensive and you might need it later. Store all topsoil at the far corner of the site where it won't be in the way. Consider keeping subsoil to make up levels at a later date. Remember, it will be even more expensive to buy it back and remember also that the heaps will shrink to a fraction of their size.

SHOP AROUND FOR MATERIALS

5 Open accounts with as many builders' merchants as you can and shop around for the best prices. Don't be afraid to play one off against another. If you have a bill of quantities – or they are prepared to prepare one – compare the cost for the whole job lot rather than for individual items and then go back to the cheapest and haggle the prices down on the anomalies. If you live close to the Channel ports, think about buying luxury items from abroad at a fraction of the costs.

CONSIDER SERVICES

6 The cost of services may, at first, seem beyond your control. But there are things you can do to mitigate them. If the connection to the mains sewer is in the road and your neighbours have a manhole close to your boundary, paying them for the slight inconvenience of connecting to it might cost a fraction of the alternative. Think carefully about the position of meter boxes and the entry point for the water so that you can utilise the same trenches for all of the services.

STICK TO A TRUSSED ROOF

7 Using pre-fabricated trusses is nearly always going to be cheaper than having to construct roofs on site from assorted lumber. The labour costs will be lower as the roof can be 'slung' in less time. The material costs may be slightly more but if you can rationalise the design to use the same size trusses on all roof planes, this may work out cheaper. If you are going to occupy the roof consider the use of 'attic' trusses, but remember that you may well need a crane to get them up onto the wallplate and more men to position them.

DON'T HAGGLE WITH LABOUR PRICES

8 Other than finding the plot and getting the planning permission, there's probably no greater worry for the self-builder than getting the right builders. But don't let that fear stampede you into taking the first price. Try to get at least three quotations. Take advice beforehand and use the services of the companies that can quantify the costs. Ask other self-builders in the area for the names of those who've done good work for them at reasonable prices. Never try to haggle over labour or supply-and-fix prices. They'll only get it back by skimping on the job.

WATCH OUT FOR EXPENSIVE EXTERNAL MATERIAL CHOICES

★ **9** One of the biggest factors in the cost of building will be the choice of the external materials. Changing from one brick to a more expensive one will add a little to the material costs but is unlikely to reflect on the labour costs. Changing from brick to natural stone will not only push up the material costs but will entail a dramatic increase in the labour costs and considerably extend the timeframe of the building. The choice of roof coverings will also affect costs as stone slabs might mean having to add structural support to the roof.

"THE SUPPOSED SAVINGS OF CHOOSING RENDER OVER BRICK ARE EASILY WIPED OUT."

Ceramic floor tiles might not necessarily work out more expensive.

WATCH OUT FOR FALSE ECONOMIES

★ **10** **Switching from a brick exterior finish to a rendered blockwork finish may, at first sight, seem to be the cheaper option. But when you have to add in two more weather-dependent trades – the plasterer and the decorator – in order to finish and when the scaffolding has to stay up longer, these 'savings' are wiped out. Choosing softwood timber windows might be what you want. But if it's to save money, consider the fact that they may have to be decorated. Ceramic tiles (above) on the floor may seem more expensive than carpet or vinyl — but you'll get the VAT back.**

MAINTAIN CONTINUITY

★ **11** **'Time is money' is a well-known phrase and it has no greater significance than in the building industry. For those on borrowed money in rented accommodation, every extra month adds to the costs. Learn the sequences of events on a building site. Plan ahead and pre-empt the requirements for both labour and materials. Above all, avoid waiting time and labour standing idle on site because of a lack of materials or because they're waiting for another trade to complete. Make yourself aware of the lead-in times for materials and keep in touch with labour that is off-site.**

★ **12**

STAY AWAY FROM FADS THAT DON'T TRANSLATE INTO VALUE

It's all too easy to get carried away with innovations and extras that can be built into a home. But never lose sight of the budget and always relate expenditure to the final value of the home. Having a heat pump, solar or photovoltaic panels or a central vacuum might be important to you, but they will put the costs up and they are unlikely to translate into increased property value. When it comes to selling into a largely uninitiated market, they may even detract from it. Be careful about personalising things too much unless you're planning to stay forever.

★ **13**

AVOID HIGH PROFESSIONAL CHARGES

Negotiating prices with professionals such as architects and solicitors may seem daunting. But in the big picture of your new home, they are just one more trade. There's no need to feel daunted by their sense of self-importance. It's all too easy to get sucked into believing that a choice other than the one being presented to you is somehow going to spoil the whole project. Experience is always a good thing but flair and imagination are just as important. Remain in the driving seat and always relate professional fees to the overall budget for your new home.

WATCH OUT FOR SPECIFICATION OVERRUNS

14 There is universal dissatisfaction at the level of services in many 'off the shelf' homes and most self-builders want to increase the number of things like power points and lighting. But think about it carefully. It's very easy to double or even treble the amount of an original quotation for a fairly basic specification. Yet in many self-built homes, there are too many plugs, switches and lights that hardly ever get used. Think about your use of each room and the position of furniture and appliances. Most of the cost overruns on a self-build site are elective.

15

BATHROOMS LOOK GREAT FOR LESS

Shop around for sanitaryware and go for eye-catching design. This doesn't have to be expensive if you keep away from specialist upmarket outlets – you can probably find the same or its equivalent at your local builders' merchants or out-of-town store. Going to the Continent and getting them direct can mean a huge saving. For those who want a traditional feel to their bathrooms, it pays to visit reclamation companies for bargains at a fraction of the cost. Mix cheaper wall tiles with expensive dado or border tiles.

REMEMBER: KITCHENS DON'T HAVE TO COST A FORTUNE

16 The kitchen is undoubtedly one of the main selling points of any new home and it goes a long way towards establishing its value. But you don't have to spend a fortune in order to get a good-looking kitchen with that important 'wow' factor. Don't be afraid to mix and match expensive with economy. Choose the door and drawer colours and textures to maximise the feeling of space within the room. Go for slightly more expensive worktops and don't forget that even the most expensive wall tiles won't add much to the total cost: you don't need too many.

"YOU COULD LOSE AS MUCH AS YOU ARE TRYING TO SAVE BY ATTEMPTING DIY."

TARGET YOUR DIY

17 If you want to be physically involved in the building of your new home and you are as good as or better than most tradesmen at a particular task, then by all means do it. But if you're not that good or you're slow, you could lose as much as you're trying to save and delay other tradesmen. Worse still, you could be so busy working on site that you let the all-important management slip. Try to confine your DIY activities to trades that can follow on from moving in, such as decoration and the finer details of the gardening.

CO-ORDINATE THE PLANT AND SCAFFOLDING

19 **Most scaffolding is hired on the basis of a minimum ten-week period with a swingeing extra for each week thereafter. Always plan to get the scaffolding in as late as possible, when you get to halfway up the ground floor windows, even if you have to hire in trestles and boards beforehand. Keep the job going to make sure that you get the roof on and the scaffolding down within the initial hire period. If diggers are on site for one task, consider whether they can use up the day by shifting spoil, making up levels or moving materials.**

AVOID CHANGING YOUR MIND

20 It's your new home and you'll want things to be as you want. But if that means coming home every night and changing things that will add time to the job, it'll start to cost more and the labour will get fed up. Think things out carefully beforehand. Walk through the home in your mind. If one trade takes longer because you've changed your mind, another trade may have to go away and you'll lose continuity. Always make your mind up in time and be aware of the lead-in times for items of choice and hard-to-come-by tradesmen.

KEEP A TIDY SITE

18 It may seem mundane but, apart from keeping on top of the management of the site, the most important task you can undertake is simply keeping the site tidy. Most wastage on site can be attributed to untidiness when materials get lost or broken. Sweeping up the bits of mortar from the oversite may take a few minutes each evening, but leaving them to harden may mean the second fix trades taking a day and half to hack it up later. Keeping the walkways clear prevents accidents. Covering the sand and putting the cement in the dry avoids unnecessary waste.

"STICK TO THE PLAN. CHANGING YOUR DESIGN AS YOU GO ALONG WILL ADD SIGNIFICANTLY TO THE BUILD COST."

Buying materials yourself can be a daunting task for the novice self-builder, but is the best way to ensure you are saving as much money as possible. Jason Orme explains where to start.

HOW TO BUY MATERIALS

BUILDING MATERIALS — everything from the cement, blocks and roof tiles that form your house's shell to the flooring, kitchen and lights that make it a liveable space — account for around half of a self-builder's expenditure. As a result, getting good deals is critical to building a house to a modest budget.

Time was that the majority of self-builders were happy to leave the purchasing of the materials to their builder or package supplier — perhaps going along to the merchants on a Saturday morning to accompany their builder and make a choice on a bathroom suite. These days, as more and more self-builders — buoyed by reading books such as this — feel confident enough to get involved with the specification of not just the finishes but also the key materials, they are having to take on one of the builder's traditional key tasks and deal directly with the suppliers ('Are you retail or trade?' 'Er…'), negotiate quantities and discounts on their own behalf and generally behave like they know exactly what they are talking about. Most builders, of course, have a long-standing relationship with their merchants and could quite easily buy in, on your behalf, everything from tiles to taps, all at a comfortable discount.

There are difficulties with ordering materials directly. For a start, builders tend to like the control they have over ordering — for three reasons. Firstly, they can take control over the delivery process and ensure they get stock when they need it. Secondly, and more worryingly for the self-builder, they are only likely to specify items for your project

Most DIY sheds work on a cash upfront basis. They don't operate accounts and barely do deliveries.

➤

★ **DEALING WITH THE KEY RETAILERS**

There is a range of large retailers — known in the building trade as 'sheds' — that offers a multitude of products to the self-builder. Wickes is perhaps the most building-orientated, as can be seen by the number of local jobbing builders parked outside with vans on a Monday morning. It offers timber, joinery items, lintels, plasterboard and most of the key construction materials apart from blocks and bricks. It also offers a useful range of essential supplies from decking and fencing to a surprisingly attractive range of paint, kitchens and bathroom fittings. It straddles the two worlds of building and home improvement and prices are pretty keen.

The more well-known retail park home improvement stores — B&Q, Homebase and the like — offer a much more retail-driven experience and for most self-builders they are only really useful towards the end of the project. Kitchen-driven retailers such as Magnet and MFI offer a free design service and prices are usually highly negotiable. Most branches of Magnet have trade counters (where you should present yourself) while MFI has a highly regarded contract brand called Howdens which offers cheap and cheerful kitchens for knockdown prices. Again, many of the smaller specialists in the key areas — kitchens and bathrooms — actually offer the best value, highest quality items, often supplying kitchens fully made up, which cuts down on labour costs.

★

PAYMENT

While most builders are able to establish credit terms with materials suppliers, for most self-builders their relationships with suppliers are likely to be little more than one-offs. As a result, most insist on a pro forma – upfront – payment. This applies equally from kitchen tiles to kitchens, despite the sums involved. With those suppliers that you can convince you will give repeat business, credit terms are much more likely. You will need to provide bank details and introduce yourself as a self-builder — the leading merchants, Travis Perkins, Jewsons and Build Center, have all courted the self-build market in recent years and will be more than happy to accommodate you. Credit terms are either 30 or 60 days, and VAT invoices are sent out a few days after delivery.

DEALING DIRECT

The building world is still very much set up in the traditional model of supplier/distributor, so for the self-builder who is new to the market it can be a little confusing. For instance, suppliers of many of the leading 'construction' materials, such as lintels and membranes, will not sell directly to the public and even those that do will tend to be undercut by their suppliers. For the most part, establishing a relationship with one merchant for the majority of your products is the most sensible arrangement – not least because it standardises your cash-flow.

MANY OF THE MAJOR MERCHANTS DO NOT HAVE ONLINE ORDERING FACILITIES, SO IT'S NOT POSSIBLE TO ORDER 3,000 BLOCKS, 10,000 BRICKS AND SO ON SIMPLY FROM YOUR ARMCHAIR.

The internet can take the legwork out of the search for 'softer' products – everything from plumbing and electrics supplies, windows and mouldings to switches, radiators and showers.

that they are comfortable with – which isn't always necessarily the items you want to be choosing. Anything out of the ordinary tends to get branded 'foreign rubbish', with dark mutterings about how long it will take to fit. If you're buying it, you have to take responsibility for ensuring it can be fitted by your builder. Thirdly, the builder is likely to be a little put out at missing out on the possibility of putting their inevitable markup onto the materials they buy on your behalf (in the same way that they would do for subcontract labour they organise).

An understanding of what it is you require, in what quantities, how it will be fitted and when it needs to be delivered are all critical when taking on ordering materials. Happily, there is a massive variety of outlets offering products to the self-builder.

THE INTERNET

Over 75% of the UK's households have internet access and shopping for materials has much appeal for self-builders, both novice and experienced. The internet is easily searchable through one of the major search engines and you are almost guaranteed to find information on a supplier that you can in turn contact through other means or, more preferably, buy directly from its own website. You can find almost anything and, even better, with the anonymity of armchair surfing you can look closely at materials, technical specifications and sizes. Most importantly, prices are clearly displayed, so you know that everyone is paying the same as you. Delivery is usually fast and often free on orders over a modest value; an email confirmation is usually sent, while a VAT invoice normally arrives in the post a few days after delivery.

There is a range of sites suitable for buying most building materials, although many of the major merchants do not have online ordering facilities, so, for the present time, it's not possible to order 3,000 blocks, 10,000 bricks and so on simply from your armchair. For the 'softer' materials, however – everything from plumbing and electrics supplies, windows and mouldings to switches, radiators and showers – the internet provides a host of one-stop sites and smaller outlets where time is the only barrier to getting the best deal. The most famous of these one-stop sites is Screwfix, which offers 10,000s of products at

BUYERS' TRICKS

If you are buying your own materials, it helps to know a few ins and outs of the bartering techniques that are routinely used by the building trade. Mark Brinkley – author of the Housebuilder's Bible – gives an insider's guide.

■ Start by opening accounts at all your local builders' merchants. While you are at it, give them copies of your plans and ask them to quote to supply the materials: most will be happy to oblige, though the service may be a little slow. It lets them know that you will be a substantial customer, if only for a brief period. You will probably require a bank reference but not necessarily trade references, if you don't yet have any.

■ Use specialists. Don't forget to also open accounts at tool hire shops and any other significant outlets you can envisage using, such as plumbers' merchants or electrical wholesalers. The best deals for items such as electrical goods, plumbing fittings, roofing materials and insulation rarely come from the general merchants.

■ Buying on account itself has two clear advantages. Firstly, you get credit: the normal terms are to pay at the end of the month following the month of purchase. Secondly, invoices are sent batched together, plus a monthly statement, which makes it much easier to collate paperwork – especially important if you have a VAT reclaim to make at the end of the job.

■ Use the prices you have subsequently obtained for your materials to haggle. Speak to the manager or one of the reps about the prices you have been offered and, if there are areas where the competition is cheaper, ask them to "see if they can do something". Often the business that is keenest to catch your trade will be prepared to match the best prices you have been quoted elsewhere.

■ Many products, such as joinery, PVCu pipes and guttering, sanitaryware and ironmongery are sold at discount to list price. Usually, one manufacturer's products can be substituted for another, so even if merchants supply different products, it is usually possible to switch to a supplier with a better discount. Note that you should check that the quality is the same (look for relevant BS numbers or at the detailed specification) and don't be tempted to buy similar products from two different suppliers

JOINERY IS ROUTINELY OFFERED AT 30% OFF LIST PRICE, BUT IT IS NOT UNUSUAL TO GET 40% OR EVEN 45%.

Wickes prices its building materials pretty keenly across the board and you can use its price catalogue as a yardstick to see if the prices you have been offered are competitive.

on the same job, unless you are sure there are no compatibility issues.

■ The size of the discounts varies enormously, depending on your trading record and the volume you order. However, the discounts are also highly negotiable. Joinery, for instance, is routinely offered at 30% off list price, but it is not unusual to get 40% or even 45% off if the merchant is keen for your business.

■ Many other products such as cement, plasterboard, timber and blocks don't have list prices as such and are sold at pre-arranged rates. Preferred builders will get the best rates, but again, these rates are open to negotiation. Use your leverage and the alternative quotes you have to get better rates.

■ Note that the DIY sheds such as B&Q and Wickes work on a cash upfront basis. They don't operate accounts and rarely do deliveries. They tend, therefore, not to be very useful for heavyside building materials but their prices are usually keen for finishing items such as tiles, flooring and paint. Wickes, in particular, prices its building materials pretty keenly across the board and you can use its price catalogue as a yardstick to see if the prices you have been offered are competitive.

■ Don't be fooled by half-price kitchen offers. They are always half-price. Kitchen discounts are also there to be negotiated. 50% off is just the starting point.

■ The best discounts go where the merchants have the least work to do. For instance, a house load of joinery delivered in one trip, direct from the manufacturer, will get a much better discount than windows and doors sent out in drips and drabs. If you can prepare your orders so that they can be delivered in as few trips as possible, you will benefit in terms of what you pay. In order to take advantage of this, you need to have a site capable of securely storing building materials. It's no good negotiating superb discounts if the goods then go 'walkabout' from your site.

BUYING ABOARD

A growing army of self-builders (particularly in the South-East) are joining those in search of cheap booze and food by crossing the Channel to buy building materials. A series of merchants in Northern France (predictably centered on Calais) offer a range of building materials at up to 50% discount on their UK counterparts – even on identical products that are produced in the UK! Materials that are most popular with UK shoppers include sanitaryware, flooring and joinery. UK self-builders can reclaim the VAT they pay on materials within the EU. Although some fittings may be different with Continental products (such as toilets), most competent plumbers will be able to deal with this in new build projects.

As a result of the increased level of interest from UK visitors, many of the merchants have English-speaking staff on hand to deal with any queries. Before heading to France, it pays to check out the merchants' websites to see what is on offer – and what size of van to hire!

SPECIALIST MERCHANTS

While the main merchants offer a broad range of supplies covering all sectors, if it's an unusual-sized shower trap you're after or a better selection of paving slabs, a specialist merchant is what you need. Check your local listing directories for details.

BECOME FAMILIAR WITH ONE LOCAL OUTLET AND ESTABLISH A RELATIONSHIP WITH THE STAFF — YOU SHOULD THEN BE ABLE TO WIELD A GREATER LEVERAGE ON DISCOUNT TERMS.

competitive prices on a next-day delivery service and, for larger orders, offers fully quantifiable discounts. Its catalogue is a genuine must-have for self-builders and renovators – at the very least it will give you a decent starting point for prices. While it has traditionally targeted itself towards the small builder and DIYer, there are signs that, perhaps due in part to the fact that the company was recently bought out by B&Q, it is moving away from its own-brand small fixings niche and branching out into offering quality names (such as Baumatic, Crabtree and Stoves) at low prices. Indeed, Screwfix is perhaps best known in self-build circles today for its low-cost, high-style towel radiators.

Many of the smaller-scale retailers operate in niches, such as lighting or flooring. In many cases, the self-builder will quickly be able to compare prices between them – but be sure to check that some of the smaller outlets have enough quantity in stock. This self-builder is still waiting for five garden lights some nine weeks after having ordered them from one lighting supplier, only to be told they are due in yet another month.

Choosing fittings through one of the larger high street suppliers is very easy, with bathrooms and flooring being particularly well served. Purchases that require some design work, such as kitchens, still require a personal showroom visit – although, surprisingly, buying paint online is proving very successful.

It is perhaps the second-hand market for which the internet is most renowned, with eBay and a range of other specific building-related sites giving varied levels of success for the self-builder: architrader.com is one of the better examples, selling a wide range of materials mainly in the salvage sector; eBay is effectively an online marketplace for unused or second-hand goods where interested parties can bid for the products. It can throw up some great bargains – many DIYers put unwanted over-orders on the site and the keen searcher can take advantage of some good deals, with everything from windows to floor tiles covered. The amount of materials on the site is now so vast that it is possible to search by brand name (for example, 'Porcelanosa floor tiles') and for a handful of options to come up. Unfortunately, eBay can also be very time-consuming and the increased intrusion of commercial retailers selling their wares at not-very-bargain prices (for example in the flooring sector) makes it a slightly unsatisfying process for the self-builder.

More interesting for self-builders are the specialist websites such as ebuild.co.uk, which offers a useful classified section for unwanted materials, and the internet arm of the reclamation organisation Salvo, which has a very useful directory perfect for people in search of reclaimed materials.

THE TAKE-OFF

The 'take-off' is another name for the full list of materials and quantities that will go into the construction of your new house. It's obviously essential for purchasing construction materials such as blocks, lintels, membranes and so on, and you can get hold of one either by employing a quantity surveyor to come up with one on your behalf; by using one of the estimating software systems such as HBXL or Easy Price Pro; by using one of the builders' merchants free take-off offers; or by estimating it yourself. To an extent, the accuracies of the take-off will diminish as you get to the end of the list because all are based on estimates of the house size and layout.

Estimating programmes such as HBXL and Easy Price Pro offer a full estimating package, usually through an Excel-based system, which will quantify your project for you and tie into merchants' price books (Jewsons, in the case of HBXL). As a result, it is also a great way of coming up with a good estimate for the build cost of the project and having a starting reference for prices. Prices of packages vary but expect to pay between £200-£600.

USEFUL CONTACTS

French Builders' Merchants: Castrorama: www.castorama.fr; Leroy Merlin: www.leroymerlin.fr; Lapeyre: www.lapeyre.fr; **Estimating Software:** EstimatorXpress: 0870 850 2444 www.hbxl. co.uk; **Easy Price Pro:** 0845 612 4747 www.easypricepro. com; **Merchants:** B&Q: www. diy.com; Wickes: 0500 300328 www.wickes.co.uk; Screwfix: 0500 414141 www.screwfix.com; Jewson: www.jewson.co.uk; Travis Perkins: www.travisperkins.co.uk; Build Center: www.build-center. co.uk

★ BUYING FROM BUILDERS' MERCHANTS

There are three national builders' merchants – Travis Perkins, Jewson and Build Center. These are joined by up to 50 established regional builders' merchants 'chains' who are well-known in their areas of operation; in addition, there are many more single outlets. They were traditionally intimidating places for most outsiders but these days self-builders form a vital part of their custom base so are treated pretty well. Become familiar with one local outlet and establish a relationship with the staff – you should be able to wield a greater leverage on discount terms, and, of course, most discounts are volume led. Credit terms will be either 30 or 60 days.

PACKAGE COMPANIES

If the thought of buying materials directly is too much to bear, then you should strongly consider approaching one of the many package companies. They have established relationships over several years with many of the leading materials suppliers and you, as a customer, will benefit from any discounts they can negotiate. Bear in mind that you will be paying a premium for the package supplier to negotiate on your behalf, but the savings can still be significant. In any instance, remember that as a customer you have a lot of power to wield in terms of both negotiating discounts and ensuring you get ★ what you want. ■

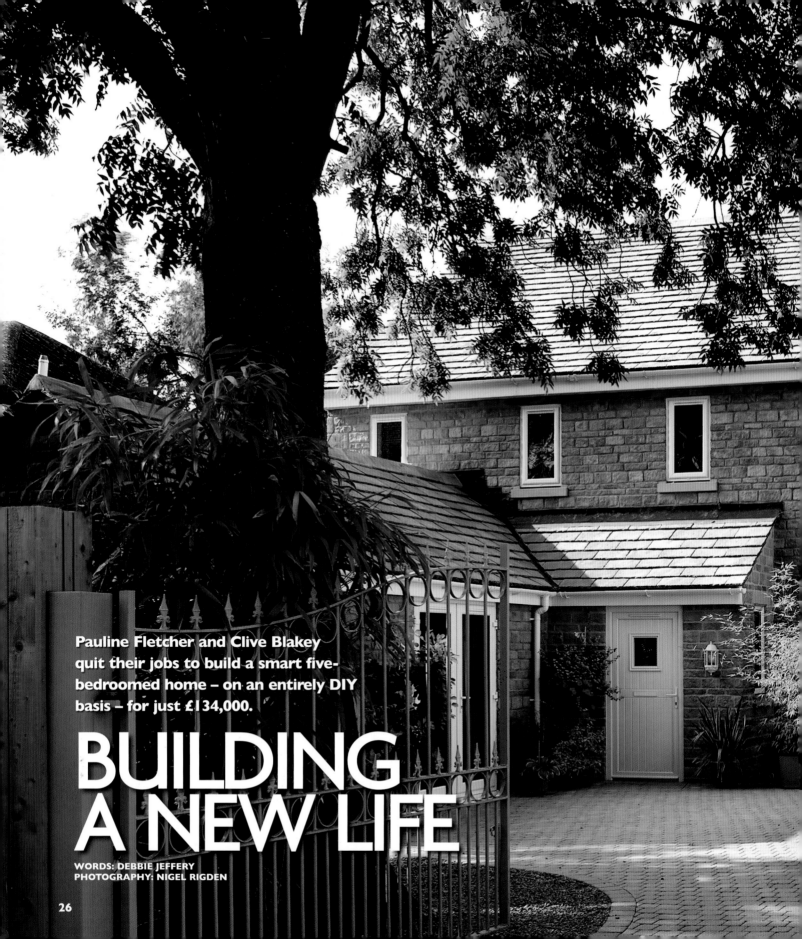

Pauline Fletcher and Clive Blakey
quit their jobs to build a smart five-
bedroomed home – on an entirely DIY
basis – for just £134,000.

BUILDING
A NEW LIFE

WORDS: DEBBIE JEFFERY
PHOTOGRAPHY: NIGEL RIGDEN

26

HOMEBUILDING & RENOVATING MAGAZINE

AWARDS 2006

BEST VALUE FOR MONEY

ONCE WE'D DECIDED to fulfil a long-standing ambition to build our own home, we handed in our notice at work and kissed goodbye to the security of monthly pay cheques," says Pauline Fletcher. "After spending every holiday, evening and weekend for five years renovating a Victorian house, we planned to take on an even more ambitious project and, because we wanted to do most of the work ourselves, we knew that it would be almost impossible to achieve this on a part-time basis."

Pauline and her partner, Clive Blakey, were both teachers and – apart from the experience they had gained from their previous renovation – had little practical building knowledge. Clive had served an old-fashioned apprenticeship as a cabinetmaker and knew that he would be able to undertake all of the joinery, including ➤

"WE MOVED INTO THE HOUSE ONCE WE HAD FITTED THE WINDOWS, BUT THERE WERE NO WASHING FACILITIES SO WE TOOK SHOWERS OUT IN THE GARDEN USING A WATERING CAN."

making the staircase, but the couple also planned to tackle everything from roofing to electrics and plumbing, fitting windows and doors, painting, tiling and installing the kitchen and bathrooms.

"It took ages to find our small orchard plot in Frome, which had already been granted Outline Planning Permission," Clive explains. "We managed to secure the land by making an offer prior to the auction, and when we first bought it we were still working as teachers and didn't start the build for a year or so."

Rather than employing an architect, the couple decided to design the new house themselves, and Pauline set about producing drawings based around a simple box shape which she then extended with a studio annexe and a long utility room to maximise the plot. Despite the fact that this was going to be a low-budget build, the property extends over three storeys and boasts five bedrooms, four bathrooms and a detached double garage and hobbies room. There's a spacious sitting room, an open plan kitchen/family living room, and the first floor landing is large enough to become a sixth bedroom should the need arise.

"We paid an architectural technologist to draw up my scaled plans and the elevations, and the design sailed through planning," says Pauline. "We then employed contractors to build the foundations and brickwork, and to

manufacture and fit the roof trusses. When the bricklayers had finally built up to the gable ends, we were left to carry on the build ourselves. Looking at those massive attic trusses waiting to be covered in the dark and wet of winter, we felt abandoned and completely alone."

Clive and Pauline used an electric hoist to transport over 1,000 roof tiles up onto the scaffolding at eaves level. Clive then settled himself on the roof slope, while Pauline tucked each large tile under her arm and carefully walked up the roof battens – placing the tile before him. Once this had been nailed into position, Clive then shunted himself along ready for the next one, while Pauline continued trekking up and down the roof.

The couple confess that working long hours in such close proximity stretched their relationship to the limit, and the sparks flew. They even took to walking their dog in relays to maximise the man-hours spent working on site and to ensure a little time away from one another during the day.

"Of course there were low points," admits Pauline. "We moved into the house once we had fitted the windows, but there were no washing facilities so we ended up taking showers out in the back garden using a watering can. The house was freezing and we would eat in bed just to keep warm."

All decisions regarding the new house were design-conscious and budget-led, with many fittings found on eBay. A large curved shower in the main ▶

The spacious
separate sitting
room is a more
formal space for
entertaining.

"IT REALLY IS SAD THAT WE AS A NATION ARE SO SCARED OF TRYING OUR HAND AT PRACTICAL SKILLS."

The kitchen is an ex-display model which has been painted and fitted with legs, handles and worktops. In total, it cost them an incredibly modest £1,403.

One of the best bargains has to be the couple's ex-display kitchen, which cost them just £1,000. Pauline and Clive sold the parts and appliances they didn't want and used the money to buy an integrated fridge and a dishwasher on eBay. They made cupboard legs and two extra doors, hand-painted the cabinets and replaced the worktop, sink, taps and knobs to create a simpler, more contemporary finish. Once Clive had fitted everything and the VAT was reclaimed, the final total, including appliances, was a mere £1,403.

"We spent two years building the house and purposefully didn't go out socialising or take holidays so that we could spend all of our time working on site," says Pauline. "People occasionally popped in to see how we were doing, and the question was usually 'When will you be finished, then?' to which our answer was always 'Dunno!' Not only did we have no time scale planned but there was no set budget either – we simply decided to buy good-quality materials at the lowest possible price by shopping around, paying for materials out of savings rather than taking out a mortgage."

Ultimately, the final build cost for the house – which includes such luxuries as solid ash staircases and floors, vaulted ceilings and under-tile heating in the bathrooms – was a mere £134,000. Admittedly, this does not include the couple's 'lost' salaries, although they did carry out additional work during the build, including restoring another house, undertaking stained glass installations and fitting kitchens and bathrooms for clients.

Once their new house was finally completed, and valued at an impressive £460,000, neither Pauline nor Clive wanted to return to teaching. Instead, Pauline now works as a designer, specialising in interiors and stained glass, and Clive is a kitchen and bathroom fitter. The couple also plan to build another house in the near future – but this time it will be far smaller and easier to maintain, with ultra-low running costs. Once again they will be undertaking the majority of the work themselves, and simply do not understand why more self-builders don't follow their lead.

"Given the huge amount of information and help available from manufacturers, it really is sad that we as a nation are so scared of trying our hand at practical skills," states Pauline. "We're encouraged to leave it to the experts when there's so much more we could be doing for ourselves. All the information's out there, you just need to be prepared to look. Not only does it save money but you also get a real sense of satisfaction in what you have accomplished. To build your own house is the ultimate achievement." ■

bathroom had been used in a photo shoot for the Trevi catalogue and was left with the photographer – who charged the couple £255 – while the second-hand gates cost £280. These were originally painted black, but a coat of pale green Hammerite has given them a whole new lease of life and created a stylish and imposing entrance.

"Driving to collect our purchases gave us some time away from the house, which made it feel almost like an outing," laughs Clive. "Every time we made a saving we saw this as payment for all our hard work. Being thrifty is now often seen as rather an old-fashioned virtue, but it really was the key to our success."

JUDGES' SUMMARY

HOMEBUILDING & RENOVATING MAGAZINE AWARDS 2006 BEST VALUE FOR MONEY

Self-building has certainly been a life-changing experience for Clive and Pauline – not only has it resulted in new careers for them both, but by building a new house for such a staggeringly small amount (well under half what most self-builders would expect to pay) this brave couple have ratcheted themselves many large rungs up the property ladder in one swift step. A remarkable financial return belies the craft and finesse Clive and Pauline put into every aspect of the design and construction of the house.

SECOND FLOOR

GROUND FLOOR

FIRST FLOOR

FLOORPLAN

As well as a formal sitting room on the ground floor, the kitchen is open to an informal living room. The first and second floors feature five bedrooms and three bathrooms.

FACT FILE

Names: Pauline Fletcher and Clive Blakey
Professions: Stained glass designer and kitchen/bathroom fitter
Area: Somerset
House type: Five-bedroomed, three-storey house
House size: 287m²
Build route: Selves as project managers
Finance: Private
Construction: Brick and block
Warranty: NHBC Solo for SelfBuild
Build time: Sept '03-Dec '05
Land cost: £70,000
Build cost: £134,000
Total cost: £204,000
Current value: £460,000
Cost/m²: £467

56%
COST SAVING

Cost Breakdown:

Fees	£7,269
Utilities	£2,970
Foundations	£16,725
Blockwork (materials and labour)	£38,307
Roofing	£15,719
Windows and doors	£6,304
Electrics	£3,639
Insulation	£2,506
Plastering	£5,745
Driveway	£4,037
Flooring	£7,269
Consumables	£642
Paint	£2,423
Carpentry and joinery	£3,313
Nails, screws, ironmongery	£1,125
Kitchen units, appliances etc.	£1,403
Rear garden	£1,223
Office costs	£86
Perimeter fencing	£2,198
Staircases	£1,160
Interior tiling	£2,150
Tool hire and scaffolding	£5,941
Tools/equipment	£1,129
Utility room units and worktop	£374
TOTAL	**£133,657**

USEFUL CONTACTS

Bricklayers Tony and Barrie Clifford: 01985 212645/01985 300828 **Truss erectors** TEC: 01985 847367 **Plastering** Eddie Goodenough: 01225 762869 **Kitchen/bathrooms** Clive Blakey: 01373 455558 **Groundworks** Tim Davis: 01985 840669 **Stained glass** Pauline Fletcher: 07845 979854 www.fantasticglass.co.uk **Windows and doors** Frameworks: 01225 766408 **Ceramic tiles** Tileflair: 0117 960 9800 **Building materials** Sydenhams: 01985 213505 **Aggregates** Nigel Charlton: 01373 471505 **Pyroguard glass** CGI International: 01942 710720 **Bricks and tiles** Bradstone: 01285 646884 **Paving blocks** Brett: 01509 817187

ON THE MONEY

WORDS: HAZEL DOLAN PHOTOGRAPHY: JEREMY PHILLIPS

Sean and Tracey Duggan have built an attractive traditional-style home for just £480/m².

Tracey visited designer kitchen companies for inspiration, but baulked at paying high prices, commissioning a local company to make their mix of oak and hand-painted furniture.

The windows facing the green are wooden sliding sashes. Elsewhere, the Duggans used PVCu. Old Clamp Blend handmade bricks were used for their random colour.

SEAN AND TRACEY Duggan started married life in a house they had bought as a shell and completely designed inside. Within two years, they had bought a plot next door to it and built their second home from scratch. Finding a third project proved to be a long waiting game, but as soon as they saw a 3/4 acre site in an attractive village on the edge of York, they knew the search was over.

"We were actively looking for 12 years for the right piece of land," says Tracey. "It was just by sheer luck that we came across this one. It's very rural, with views of fields at the back and the village green at the front, and that's what appealed to us. It's also in the catchment area for the school we wanted for our daughters Eden and Ceara. It all just fell into place."

The plot, which is in a Conservation Area, falls within former farm land, and had to be cleared of old pig buildings, stables and an orchard. Its size was a real bonus and a rare find within easy reach of York. The Duggans were confident the conservation officer at Selby Council would approve of many of their ideas, including the use of handmade brick and slate,

and successfully fought their corner on other elements of their design. They had seen other new builds in the village with plastic rather than traditional cast iron guttering, and electric roller shutters for the garages, instead of doors.

Permission in place, they were ready to go. Sean runs his own property development company and was able to keep labour costs to the minimum and use trusted contacts to carry out the site work. Significant savings were made on architect's drawings, completed by Sean's father, a retired builder, and plumbing, where Sean called in a favour from his brother, Craig. His own role was hands-on too, beginning with clearing the site. "Our first priority when we got the building plot was to make a play area for the children in the back garden, so that when we came to work here at the weekends they had somewhere to play. We didn't build the house first, we built a tree house and a trampoline."

While the windows facing the green had to be wooden sliding sashes, they were free to use PVCu for the rest, carefully matching the design so the difference is scarcely noticeable. After careful research, they chose ➤

"I WANTED CHARACTER FOR THE ROOF TOO – DIFFERENT HEIGHTS AND GABLES SO IT DIDN'T LOOK FLAT AND UNIFORM. I SPENT A LOT OF TIME PLANNING THE OVERHANG AND THE DETAIL."

Sean and Tracey created an impressive entrance hall (right) with travertine flooring, Georgian style banisters and painted panelling, made from mdf.

The Duggans commissioned a traditional stone fireplace as a focal point to their large living room.

"WE LOOKED AT OLD VICARAGES AND INTERESTING BUILDINGS AND THOUGHT WE COULD PLUCK SOME OF THESE IDEAS FOR OUR OWN HOME."

Old Clamp Blend bricks from York Handmade Brick Company for their random colour and mature appearance, and stone heads and cills to add to the visual appeal. The house roof is Chinese slate and they used Arcadia pantiles for the triple garage block. "I didn't want it to look too uniform, as though you're saying: 'Yes, it's a new build!'" Sean says. "I wanted character to the house roof too — different heights and gables so it didn't look flat and uniform. I spent a lot of time planning the overhang and the detail."

Inside, too, the priority was to add character and avoid a 'brand new' feel. "We became members of the National Trust and went round all these stately homes and got ideas," says Tracey. "We looked at old vicarages and interesting buildings and thought we could pluck some of these ideas for our own home." Many of the details, from the Georgian-style glazed cabinets built into the dining room walls, to the depth of cornice, picture rails, and style of door furniture, were inspired by their research.

In the living room they followed advice and laid Boen Parkett engineered board with a 4mm oak veneer, rather than solid oak, to avoid the risk of their new underfloor heating causing warping or splitting. In the hall and kitchen they opted for travertine. Their careful budget management, bargaining and research meant there was enough left over to indulge in a treat each: a Canadian hot tub for Tracey and a plasma TV for Sean.

Everything meets their full approval and they would definitely recommend self-build as a way to achieve a high-quality home. "As it came together, it just seemed to get better and better," says Sean. "There is nothing in the house we would change. We have plenty of light, plenty of space and I love the quirkiness of the layout. I wouldn't rule out doing it again, but only if we were moving to somewhere with more land." Tracey agrees: "We're living in the ambition that we had for so long, so it's really nice to enjoy it." ∎

BUDGET PERIOD STYLE

Building a successful traditional style new home is as much down to good research as it is expensive finishes. Getting the key features right – materials, windows, staircases – is essential, however, so if you need to build to a budget, economise on interior fittings. In this case, the owners saw a kitchen design they liked and then commissioned a cheaper copy from a local supplier.

GROUND FLOOR

FIRST FLOOR

FLOORPLAN

The layout is traditional, with a formal dining room to the front. To the rear, however, a large kitchen flows into a conservatory and playroom, while upstairs, five bedrooms and gym combine with three bathrooms.

FACT FILE

Names: Sean and Tracey Duggan
Professions: Property developer and RGN nurse
Area: York
House type: Six-bedroom house
House size: 330m^2
Build route: DIY and subcontractors
Construction: Brick and block, slate roof
Warranty: NHBC
Finance: Private and NatWest
Build time: Feb '03-Feb '04
Land cost: £189,000
Build cost: £150,000 + £10,000 garages
Total cost: £349,000
House value: £725,000
Cost/m²: £484

52% COST SAVING

Cost Breakdown:

Fees	£6,385
Service connections	£1,047
Scaffolding	£2,120
Kitchen, utility, granite, appliances	£16,500
Fireplace	£2,600
Floor finishes	£5,100
Paint	£600
Fencing	£1,900
Garage doors	£1,060
Electrics	£2,900
Subcontract labour	£21,500
Windows	£11,350
Plant hire	£3,400
Landscaping	£7,300
Electric gates	£2,400
Materials	£37,000
Hot tub	£5,200
Carpets	£4,600
Soft furnishings	£20,750
TOTAL	**£160,212**

USEFUL CONTACTS

Designer T. Duggan: 01904 720604; **Bricks** York Handmade Brick Co. Ltd: 01347 838881; **Builders** Edenvale Homes: 01904 720605; **Entrance gates** A & M Electricals: 0191 419 1519; **Fireplace** Calder Masonry: 01924 463748; **Garden design** John Ellis Design: 01904 720377; **Hot tub** Clearwater: 01904 412041; **Kitchen appliances** Butterfly Furniture: 01423 330580; **Oak flooring** Boen Parkett: 0800 458 3366; **Soft furnishings** York House Interiors: 01904 414939; **Slate tiles** Crest: 0870 241 1398; **Travertine flooring** Lapicida: 01423 501249; **Underfloor heating** Velta: 01484 860811; **PVCu Windows** Welch Glazing: 01422 376012

WISH YOU WERE HERE?

WORDS: DEBBIE JEFFERY PHOTOGRAPHY: NIGEL RIGDEN

Tim and Adrienne Sowood have built their pretty Scandinavian-inspired house on a beautiful waterside location for less than £150,000.

"OUR ARCHITECT DESCRIBES this house as 'Scandinavian with a kilt on'," laughs Tim Sowood, and it's certainly easy to see why. From the pale Swedish wooden floors to the white-painted furniture, Tim and Adrienne's new home has a distinctly Scandinavian feel, despite the fact that it is actually located on the north shore of Loch Alsh in the Scottish Highlands. Situated on this enviable coastal site, the Nordic-style property enjoys views of 13th century Eilean Donan Castle and has proved to be the ideal place for the Sowoods to enjoy their active retirement.

"We were living in a village on the outskirts of Manchester and our cottage had all of the usual problems associated with old properties," Tim explains. "Realising that we couldn't afford to retire and carry on paying our mortgage, we decided to try and find a new home which would leave us mortgage-free. We were rather ➤

Siberian larch weatherboarding has been finished with three coats of translucent white stain and fixed vertically at ground floor level, with the timbers laid horizontally above – an idea copied from modern Swedish homes.

White walls, pale pine floorboards and simple painted furniture create the Scandinavian country look.

tired of old houses and wanted to live by the water, but we knew that we would need to move away from the area to find exactly what we wanted for the right price."

The couple travelled further and further north until they eventually discovered the overgrown piece of land in Ross-Shire where they would ultimately build their new house. "There were only a few properties dotted along the shoreline, and at first we thought that it was a bit too far from friends and family – although the constant stream of visitors has since disproved this," says Tim. "We'd viewed so many dark and dismal houses that starting from scratch with a new build seemed like the perfect solution. We both enjoy orienteering, and had previously travelled to Scotland many times, so finding a plot right by the water with Outline Planning Permission and such incredible views was just too good to ignore."

When it came to designing a new house, the Sowoods had very definite ideas about what they wanted. The Nordic way of life has influenced design throughout the world and Adrienne, a retired head teacher, was particularly inspired by the Swedish homes she had seen on holidays, including a school exchange visit to Stockholm.

"We explored various styles of houses and visited Skansen, the open-

"WE LOOKED AT VARIOUS KITS, BUT IN THE END OUR FRAME WAS BUILT LOCALLY IN A WORKSHOP."

The kitchen was purchased from Ikea for £2,700 and is offset by a Wedgwood blue Aga and European maple worktops.

air museum in Stockholm, as well as Carl Larsson's famous house in Sundborn," she says. "We then contacted Frank Burstow – an architect who had previously designed some Swedish-style houses in Scotland – and showed him pictures of the kind of light and airy buildings we liked."

These pictures included the beautifully crafted wooden houses dotted throughout the Swedish landscape, many of which are set in woods and beside lakes – often coming with their own private jetty. "I've always been a great believer in timber frames, so there was never any question about the type of construction we would use," says Tim, a former civil engineer. "We looked at various kits, including imported timber frames, but in the end our frame was built locally in a workshop by a joiner who was also our builder's brother."

The finished structure combines all of the Swedish elements the Sowoods desired with the planners' request for traditional dormer windows. "It's described as a one-and-three-quarter-storey house," says Tim. "A one-and-a-half-storey house is where the eaves start at first floor level, but here we have a one-metre-high vertical wall before the roof begins to slope, which means that you can sit up in bed without banging your head!"

The entrance facade of the property looks onto a quiet lane and incorporates small-paned windows, but the rear of the T-shaped house overlooks the loch and mountains beyond and is extensively glazed, with a covered balcony sheltering under the overhanging roof of the master bedroom. Below this, a conservatory opens through two sets of glazed doors from the living room, which is open plan to the dining area and ➤

A glazed conservatory leads off from the sitting area, drawing light into the open plan living spaces.

The master bedroom opens onto a spacious balcony overlooking Loch Alsh. Below: An open-tread staircase leads up from the dining area and enables light to filter between the floors.

Living so far from their site meant that the Sowoods were unable to oversee the build themselves, and instead employed their architect to undertake the project management on their behalf. Tim admits that he would have loved to become more involved, but had to make do with frequent site visits, armed with long lists.

Throughout the build, Tim and Adrienne were conscious of their ultimate goal to ensure that they would move to Scotland without the need for a mortgage, and chose their materials carefully with this in mind – keeping extremely strict accounts records. With a budget of under £150,000, IKEA proved the perfect source for several pieces of furniture and the couple have also customised certain existing items by painting them to suit their predominantly white Scandinavian country-style interiors.

The stained softwood windows are a major feature of the house and the distinctive windows in the master bedroom have been designed to follow the slant of the balcony roof. Some of the glazing is shaded by plain and striped blinds and muslin swags, although many windows have been left completely bare – once more developing the essence of Swedish style. "We face south-east towards the loch, so the sun streams into our bedroom in the morning, but we don't mind not having any curtains," Tim remarks.

The Scottish and Nordic climates are not dissimilar, with long dark winters, and the white walls and furniture, offset with a smattering of traditional blue gingham check, help to maximise the natural light. Bleached pine flooring, imported from Sweden and laid over underfloor heating, sets the scene throughout the property – which has proved to be so warm that the Sowoods rarely feel the need to light their cast iron woodburning stove.

Once the house was completed, Tim was able to retire and the couple began their new life in the Scottish Highlands. They have been made to feel part of the local community and Adrienne has taken up gardening and landscaped the previously barren site. The waterside location has also enabled them to buy a small boat.

"Moving here has been a life-changing adventure, but constructing our house for such a low budget would simply not have been possible without our architect and the talented craftsmen who built it for us. They took a real interest in what we were trying to achieve and worked together to make it happen." ■

kitchen beyond. The result is a light-filled interior, with three bedrooms nestling under the sloping eaves on the first floor and an additional fourth bedroom/study downstairs.

"We changed very little about the original design, although Tim did shave a metre off the width to make sure that the house would come in on budget," says Adrienne. "We still have plenty of space, although the conservatory – which we call the verandah – could perhaps have been a little larger as we use this room all the time because of the fantastic views."

The house faces south-east towards the loch, so the sun streams into the bedroom in the morning.

FACT FILE

Names: Tim and Adrienne Sowood
Professions: Retired
Area: Scottish Highlands
House type: Three/four-bedroom detached
House size: 200m²
Build route: Builder and subcontractors
Finance: Private
Construction: Larch-clad timber frame, slate roof
Warranty: Architect's certificate
Build time: June '03-June '04
Land cost: £30,000
Build cost: £148,000
Total cost: £178,000
Current value: £360,000
Cost/m²: £740

51%
COST SAVING

Cost Breakdown:

Site preparation and excavation	£15,000
Builder work	£10,000
Joinery/timber frame	£55,000
Plumbing and heating	£13,000
Electrics	£4,000
Roofing	£10,000
Cladding	£6,000
Decorating	£12,000
Tiling	£1,000
Flooring	£7,000
Windows	£10,000
Landscaping	£5,000
TOTAL	**£148,00**

GROUND FLOOR

FIRST FLOOR

FLOORPLAN

The ground floor is predominantly open plan, with a kitchen, dining and living area overlooking the loch. The sitting room opens into a glazed conservatory and there is a separate utility room and a study which doubles as a fourth bedroom. Upstairs, the master bedroom has a balcony and en-suite shower room; the two guest bedrooms share a bathroom, and a large storeroom has been built above the garage.

USEFUL CONTACTS

Architect Frank Burstow Architect: 01599 534040 **Builder** A Fraser Builders: 01599 511327 **Timber frame and joinery** Kenny Fraser Joinery: 01599 588221 **Underfloor heating** Rehau Ltd: 01989 762600 **Furniture, kitchen, blinds** IKEA: 020 8208 5600 **Swedish Gustavian furniture** Scumble Goosie: 01453 731305 **Superdeck wood stain** Sadolin: 01480 484262 **Aga** Aga Rayburn: 01952 642000 **Sanitaryware** Ideal Standard: 01482 346461 **Woodburner** Jøtul (UK) Ltd: 01527 506010 **Environmental septic tank** Balmoral Tanks: 01224 859100 **Wooden flooring** Baseco: 01945 587000 **Red pine windows** Treecraft Woodwork Ltd: 01862 810021 **Electrician** David Lee: 01599 511276 **Lamps** Lavender Tree: 01625 599532 **Heating design** Highland Heating Solutions Ltd: 01599 577287

FAMILY VALUES

Paul and Larisa Killoran have built a four-bedroomed family home for under £80,000 with the help of their friends and family.

WORDS: DAVID SNELL PHOTOGRAPHY: JEREMY PHILLPS

THE TROUBLE IS that we have now found the perfect plot," smiles Paul Killoran. "I'd love to build again but I don't think I could persuade Larisa to move and, if I'm honest, I'm a little reluctant myself."

We're in the kitchen of the new four-bedroomed, three-storey house that the couple have moved into exactly two years after I helped them find the plot on a Plotfinder Challenge. It's not quite finished: the driveway isn't in and the chap that's going to fix the gates and the iron railing for the front wall isn't due until next week. "But we will be finished soon," asserts Paul. Larisa catches my eye. We both know about Paul's eternal optimism, but we also know that, without it, they wouldn't be standing where they are.

The plot in Heywood stood out on the Plotfinder Challenge. The minute we saw it, we knew that this was the one. The agents had been particularly obstructive: they hadn't had details; we couldn't go to see the plot; they had someone interested. In fact, they said everything and anything they could think of to put us off.

We made contact with the vendors, part of whose back garden the plot was composed of. The plot had been sold, subject to contract, several times to various builders who'd then spent months haggling ➤

The bright modern kitchen suits family life perfectly.

over the price and arguing with the planners for a bigger house. But that wasn't what the vendors wanted. They'd had their own plans drawn up and they wanted to have some control over the impact this new house was going to have on their own.

Paul and Larisa were delighted with the houseplans. They were just what they wanted – to the delight of the vendors. Furthermore, they were prepared to pay the full asking price of £51,000 with no quibbles.

It took a few months for all the legal work to be sorted out and it wasn't until early April that they were able to start on site. Being an electrician, Paul had always reckoned that he would be able to gather labour from among his workmates, friends and family, and his costings were largely predicted upon being able to do so.

He wasn't disappointed. Many people pitched in to help: notably his friend Dave Kelly, his brother Sean and another friend, Tom. But there's a downside to pulling favours: with payment not always at full value, some chaps (not the ones mentioned) can feel that the job isn't perhaps as important as their other work. It would take all of Paul's management skills to pull everything together.

Paul was always going to have to build this house by putting a large amount of labour in himself and, obviously, doing all of the electrics, while ➤

"I ASSUMED EVERYTHING WAS CUT AND DRIED AS FAR AS THE PLANNING WAS CONCERNED WHEN, TO BE HONEST, I'D NEVER EVEN READ THE FULL CONSENT."

WE COULD HAVE CAMPED OUT IN THE HOUSE, I WASN'T PREPARED TO DO IT WITH A NEW BABY. PAUL WAS WORKING THERE EVERY EVENING AND IN WHATEVER SPARE TIME HE HAD. IN THE END, IT WASN'T UNTIL AUGUST THAT WE FINALLY MOVED IN."

holding down his own business. He realised from the start, and from knowledge of how a building site works, that he had to try to minimise the amount of time he spent chasing around after materials. "I sent the plans and a full list of materials to three separate builders' merchants," he recalls. "When they came back there were remarkable price differences, not only for individual items but, more importantly, for the total amount. Would you believe 54% between the highest and lowest?

"So, when I got the prices in I went to see the best one and told the guy that I didn't have time to fish about and that I wanted to be able to rely on them. The chap said, 'Fine,' and then introduced me to Lee Jackson, who would be my account manager. It proved to be one of the best things that happened, saving me no end of hassle.

"I wish, though, that I'd taken as much care with the paperwork.

Space-saving features such as the spiral staircase help to give the house a more airy feeling.

Because the plans of the house were just what we wanted, it had lulled me into a false sense of security, and I made a huge mistake. I assumed that everything was cut and dried as far as the planning was concerned when, to be honest, I'd never even read the full consent."

On the site there were some large trees at the back of the plot. When the building inspector came out to inspect the footings, he took one look at them and the trenches and told Paul and Larisa to hold on while he went and checked things out. When he rang back to tell them that he'd need engineer's calculations, he also had more bad news: they were in breach of a planning condition requiring them to verify the setting out before commencement of work.

Paul had to involve an engineer for the footings and the planning officer had to come out and measure from their proposed house to key points on the adjoining properties. "It taught me a lesson," says Paul. "It all worked out fine and the officers were really fair, but after that I read

everything from cover to cover before making a move."

There were some scary moments during the foundations and oversite stages, with concrete and pumps being delayed and some fairly drastic changes having to be made, but once out of the ground things progressed quite well. Some trades were good; others not so. There were three different gangs of bricklayers on site. The first gang said they'd be done in four-and-a-half weeks. "Four-and-a-half months wouldn't have seen them finished," Paul complains. "Every time I went to site it was for them to moan at me. 'When do you need the stone cills,' I asked. 'In about four weeks,' they said. Two weeks later they said they couldn't carry on without them!

"In the end I hired another gang. Then a third gang did the wall at the front, finished off the chimney and filled in the putlog holes."

On March 27, 2004, Paul and Larisa had a baby girl, Lucy. The house was by then basically habitable, but Larisa was reluctant to move in: "I said I wasn't going to move in until the drive was in," she remembers. "And although we could have camped out in the house, I wasn't prepared to do it with a new baby. Paul was working there every evening and in whatever spare time he had, and family members all pitched in to help. In the end it wasn't until August that we finally moved in."

"We had one or two hiccups," says Paul. "But to be honest, I miss the excitement of it all now it's done."

"Paul kept a lot from me, I know," Larisa admits. "But he never got disheartened – he just put things right.

I had absolute faith in him and I was right to." ∎

FACT FILE

Names: Paul and Larisa Killoran
Professions: Electrician and schoolteacher
Area: Greater Manchester
House type: Four-bed detached
House size: 160m²
Build route: Self-managed plus DIY
Finance: BuildStore
Construction: Brick and block
Build time: Apr '03-Aug '04
Land cost: £51,000
Build cost: £78,250
Total cost: £129,250
Current value: £245,000
Cost/m²: £490

48%
COST SAVING

Cost Breakdown:

Labour	£31,011
Professional fees, services and connection charges	£4,862
Materials and plant	£37,277
Driveway	£2,500
Gates and railing	£2,600
TOTAL	**£78,250**

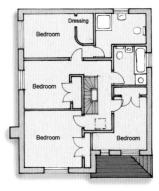

GROUND FLOOR   **FIRST FLOOR**

FLOORPLAN

The ground floor features an open plan kitchen and family room, with a dining room that can be separated off from the living room.

USEFUL CONTACTS

Structural engineers Paul Healey & Co: 01706 343961 **Plant hire** Rochdale Plant Hire: 01706 653218 **Builders' merchants** Parrs of Rochdale: 01706 656980 **Electrics** PK Electrical: 07977 107822 or 01706 368984 **Tiles** Athena Ceramics & Tilers: 0161 950 6303 **Windows** Alexandra Windows: 0161 482 2322 **Ironwork** Peniron Ornamental Ironwork: 01706 622096 or 07816 102108 **Staircase** Elite Staircases: 01926 812060

ECONOMY CLASS

WORDS: DEBBIE JEFFERY   PHOTOGRAPHY: NIGEL RIGDEN

Mike and Syvona Woods' new home enjoys the finest features available to 21st century homeowners and plenty of exciting architectural spaces – not bad for a pair of first-time self-builders on a budget of £140,000.

The house has a traditional stone frontage with cottage-style windows and a planked entrance door.

APPROACH MIKE AND Syvona Woods' house from the front and the stone walls, small windows and farmhouse-style entrance door give the distinct impression of a property which has stood on the site for a number of years. Walk around to the rear, however, and you are faced with what could be a completely different

Dark slate-effect floor tiles complement the black granite worktops in the kitchen/diner. The refrigerator is set into a wall of units in the kitchen, with three downlighters creating a curtain of light from above.

building. White render, large windows and French doors with a double-height glazed entrance vestibule pronounce that it is, in fact, a contemporary home. This curious arrangement was partly dictated by strict planning requirements for the new house, which is built on the south-facing slope of a valley in Penycae, Wales, within the Brecon Beacons National Park.

"A developer had sold off plots and was left with a portion of land sandwiched between the development and the main road," explains Mike, an architectural technologist who was keen to use his talents to design and build his own house. "We had been let down on another plot and were in the position to make an offer of £40,000 for the land, which measures 30 by 30 metres. It had been earmarked as residential development under the local plan and I was confident that we would be able to build a house. Despite the fact that it came with no formal planning permission it didn't feel like we were taking a serious risk."

The planners were keen that the Woods should build a traditional property suited to its location, with stone walling, small timber windows and natural materials typical of the Brecon Beacons. Mike was concerned that this style of house would have exceptionally dark interiors, and suggested a compromise. "I said to them 'hang on a second. I've got these fabulous, unobstructed south-facing views and you want me to build a cottage looking onto the road?' After a bit of toing and froing they ➤

"IT HAD BEEN HARD TO VISUALISE THE SPACES, BUT ONCE I COULD WALK AROUND THE HOUSE I WAS ABLE TO GET A REAL FEEL FOR HOW THEY COULD LOOK."

The large glazed rear vestibule provides a thermal store for the whole house. Glass balustrading, oak handrails and contemporary fittings give the interior a sense of luxury that belies the modest budget.

"PEOPLE OFTEN COMMENT THAT THE WINDOWS LOOK VERY SMALL, AND THAT IT MUST BE QUITE DARK, BUT INSIDE IT'S SO LIGHT AND AIRY THEY CAN'T BELIEVE IT'S THE SAME PROPERTY."

agreed that, if I did what they wanted at the front, I could do what I liked at the back."

Mike wanted to exploit passive solar gain from the sun, which shines onto the rear of the house from mid morning until evening, and designed a two-storey atrium to act as a heat store, drawing warmth into the core of the building which rises up to first floor level. This glazed space acts as a hinge for the L-shaped accommodation, which is arranged to be as open plan as possible on the ground floor.

"Apart from post coming through the letter box we never actually use the front door," explains Mike. "Everybody comes from the driveway and across the decking to the rear entrance vestibule, which flows directly into the kitchen and living areas. We hardly ever closed the lounge and kitchen doors in our old three-bedroomed semi, so it seemed like a good idea to just have large openings into these rooms instead."

With no doors to close between these spaces, heat from the sun may travel unhindered throughout the house, which has an open plan kitchen/dining room and a separate family room where Mike and ten-year-old Benjamin can chill out and play on the PlayStation. "People often comment that the windows look very small at the front of the house, and that it must be quite dark, but inside it's so light and airy they can't believe it's the same property," laughs Syvona. "Not long after we finished building we held a party, and the open plan layout really came into its own. In fact, we were

able to accommodate 25 people in just the kitchen area, with food spread out on the worktops and breakfast bar and the patio doors from the dining room opening out onto the deck."

Syvona and Mike's bedroom is located above the lounge and features French doors, fitted with safety railings, which face south towards views of farm and woodland to the River Tawe. An additional 150mm leaf of natural stone walling, combined with the cavity blockwork construction, ensures that the front north wall of the house is extremely thick and can absorb and retain heat from the evening sun. Even four-month-old Maddison's north-facing bedroom never feels cold or dark and holds a constant temperature of 75° without the need for additional heating.

A balcony with a glass balustrade is positioned above the entrance to the kitchen/diner and looks down into the glazed atrium, which has no formal function but to act as a focal point and transitional space linking the living areas. "When you walk to the top of the stairs you can't help but look out at the view," says Mike. "It catches my eye every day, and the sense of openness which the vestibule creates is the key to the whole plan."

Mike enjoyed designing the double-fronted house and was guided by the planners regarding the choice of materials, including locally quarried blue pennant stone for the north façade and the precise mix for the mortar. One planning condition which Mike and Syvona did contest, however, was the choice of oak window frames – preferring to fit PVCu instead. "The ➤

"NOT MANY LOCAL PLUMBERS HAD EXPERIENCE OF UNDERFLOOR HEATING SO WE DID MOST OF THE LABOUR OURSELVES."

vestibule and large windows would have been very expensive in hardwood, so I drove to look at some new developments in Brecon and discovered one which had used PVCu," says Mike. "We were eventually allowed to fit the same wood-effect frames, and it's virtually impossible to tell them apart from the real thing."

The Woods had bought their plot using their own funds and were able to remain living in their previous home – a 30-minute drive from the site – securing a stage payment self-build mortgage to fund the build. Mike acted as project manager, purchasing materials, employing individual subcontractors and labouring for the various trades. "A groundworker took us up to slab level, then a crew of bricklayers built up the blockwork to wall plate, a stonemason laid the stone, carpenters completed the floors and roof and a separate roofing contractor supplied and fixed the slates," he says. "Not many local plumbers had experience of underfloor heating so Syvona and I did most of the labour ourselves and then brought somebody in to complete the copper pipework and fit the boiler."

As the rooms began to take shape Syvona found it far easier to design the interiors. "It had been hard to visualise the spaces," she says, "but once I could walk around the house I was able to get a real feel for how they could look. Mike didn't like the idea of a fireplace in the lounge because it wasn't necessary as a heat source, but I wanted a focal point for the room and we agreed on a modern living flame hole-in-the-wall

model with a glass front cover, which we use for effect."

Slick and contemporary, the interiors avoid the ubiquitous all-white finishes so often seen in modern homes. Creamy-coloured natural hessian walls have been highlighted by stronger shades of warm cappuccino and burnt terracotta which, together with the ash joinery, create a warm, natural look. The couple had promised themselves granite worktops for the kitchen but baulked at the £3,000 expense. Ultimately, however, they decided that hard-wearing black granite would be an investment when compared to some of the less expensive options, and this has been complemented by dark slate-effect floor tiles. Pale ceramic tiles were chosen for the entrance vestibule with wood in the lounge, so that the various ground floor areas are visually defined by distinct changes in the flooring.

Mike and Syvona fitted their own multi-room hi-fi system which serves all major rooms, including the master bedroom and en-suite bathroom. "In theory you should be able to lie in the jacuzzi and listen to music, but I haven't yet found the time to enjoy it myself," says Mike, who admits that his desire for perfection wore him out during the build. "Our original budget was £112,000, but this grew to £140,000 – mainly due to finishes such as the tiles, ash staircase and bespoke internal doors. The house is now valued at around £300,000, though, so we have still made a 40% profit on paper, but I don't think we'll ever build again. It has taken me a long time to relax and start to enjoy the fruits of our labour." ■

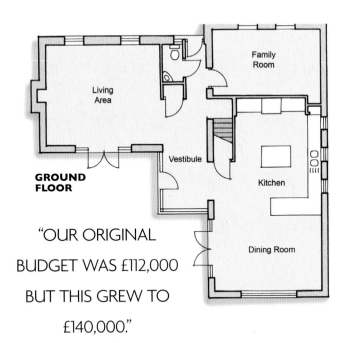

GROUND FLOOR

Living Area

Family Room

Vestibule

Kitchen

Dining Room

"OUR ORIGINAL BUDGET WAS £112,000 BUT THIS GREW TO £140,000."

FIRST FLOOR

Bedroom

Bedroom

Bedroom

Bedroom

FLOORPLAN

Designed around a double-height glazed entrance vestibule, the living room and kitchen/diner have large openings with no doors, which enable heat from the sun to pass through the building. Upstairs, four bedrooms and three bathrooms cluster in an L-shape around the atrium and a balcony looks down into the void and the entrance area below.

FACT FILE

Names: Mike and Syvona Woods
Professions: Architectural technologist and area manager of offices
Area: Swansea
House type: Four-bedroomed house with detached garage
House size: 206m^2 plus separate 50m^2 garage
Build route: Self-managed subcontractors and DIY
Construction: Rendered cavity blockwork, stone cladding, slate roof
Finance: Barclays
Build time: Nov '03-Feb '05
Land cost: £40,000
Build cost: £139,000
Total cost: £179,000
House value: £300,000
Cost/m²: £543

40%
COST SAVING

Cost Breakdown:

Building regs/warranty	£470
Shared drive/sewer diversion	£6,000
Site preparation/ substructures	£7,000
Services	£2,000
Drainage	£2,000
Superstructure	£17,000
Stone	£7,000
Roof	£7,500
Carpentry/joinery	£17,000
Windows, doors and vestibule	£13,000
UFH and plumbing	£8,000
Electrics	£4,000
Sanitaryware	£5,000
Tiling	£4,000
Internal finishes	£4,500
Decoration	£3,000
Kitchen	£4,000
Granite	£3,000
Multi-room hi-fi	£3,800
Garage	£9,000
Driveway and external works	£6,000
Decking and landscaping	£6,000
TOTAL	**£139,270**

USEFUL CONTACTS

Design and project management Concept Architectural Services: 01792 812010 **Windows** Nolan UPVC: 0845 600 9080 **Underfloor heating** Nu-Heat UK Ltd: 01404 549770 **Stone** Gwrhyd Specialist Stone Quarry: 01639 830650 **Natural slate** Harris Slate & Stone Ltd: 01267 233824 **Slate fixing** Mark Hartley: 07966 134828 **Kitchen** Sigma 3: 01443 237732 **Granite worktops** Naturiol Grates: 01792 655581 **Small plant hire** CME Plant Hire: 01639 845184 **Fireplace** Exclusive Fireplaces, Swansea: 01792 512121 **Building materials** LBS Builders' Merchant: 01639 843212 **Vintage brindled driveway pavers** Baggeridge Brick plc: 01902 880555 **Tiles** Tony's Tiles, Swansea: 01792 516055 **Glass balustrade** Windsor Glass: 01792 589761 **Doors, skirtings, etc.** Sorokin Joinery: 01792 815661 **Ironmongery** Swansea Timber & Plywood Co Ltd: 01792 655680 **Scaffolding** Orange West Scaffolding: 01639 893348 **Suspended beam and block floor** RMC Concrete Products Ltd: 0117 937 3371 **Decorator** C J Else: 01792 587215 **Multi room hi-fi** Merlin Interactive Systems: 01792 891677 **Building regulations and warranty** Total Building Control Ltd: 01792 643821 **Timber roof trusses** Forest Timber Engineering Ltd: 01792 895620 **Bath** Jacuzzi (UK) Ltd: 01782 717175 **Bathroom furniture** Roca Ltd: 01530 830080

Garry and Hayley Thomas' new hillside home was built around a busy schedule and tight budget.

WEEKEND WONDER

WORDS AND PHOTOGRAPHY: KEN PRICE

I'VE LOST COUNT of the number of people who told us we wouldn't be able to get a house on this plot of land," smiles Garry Thomas. "It was an understandable reaction considering the site was mostly hidden by brambles and trees."

Garry and his wife Hayley can afford to relax and enjoy the view from their sun lounge. They've transformed an overgrown, wedge-shaped plot of land on a steeply sloping hillside in mid Wales, into a family home for themselves and their five-year-old son Kieran.

As locals, they had known about the site for quite some time, although they weren't particularly interested until it came onto the market in 2001. "We were looking for our next step on the housing ladder. Suitable sites within our budget were few and far between in this area, so when the opportunity to buy this site arose, we jumped at it. The very sight of it would have put most people off," recalls Garry. "Having said that, at the asking price of £25,000 it was a bargain, provided we could work out how to build a house there."

The Thomases knew they could build a home from past experience. Garry is a carpenter by trade so building sites hold no fear for him. Even so, this site was a challenge even for his creative ability. "After our bid was accepted – there wasn't much serious opposition – I had to clear the site before I could begin to see how best to develop it," he remembers.

The site came with outline planning, so Hayley and Garry sketched out their ideas to get a sense of how to use the site to its best potential, especially the slope, which was a big influence on their design ideas. They anticipated needing a storey height retaining wall to support the road behind the house – which ➤

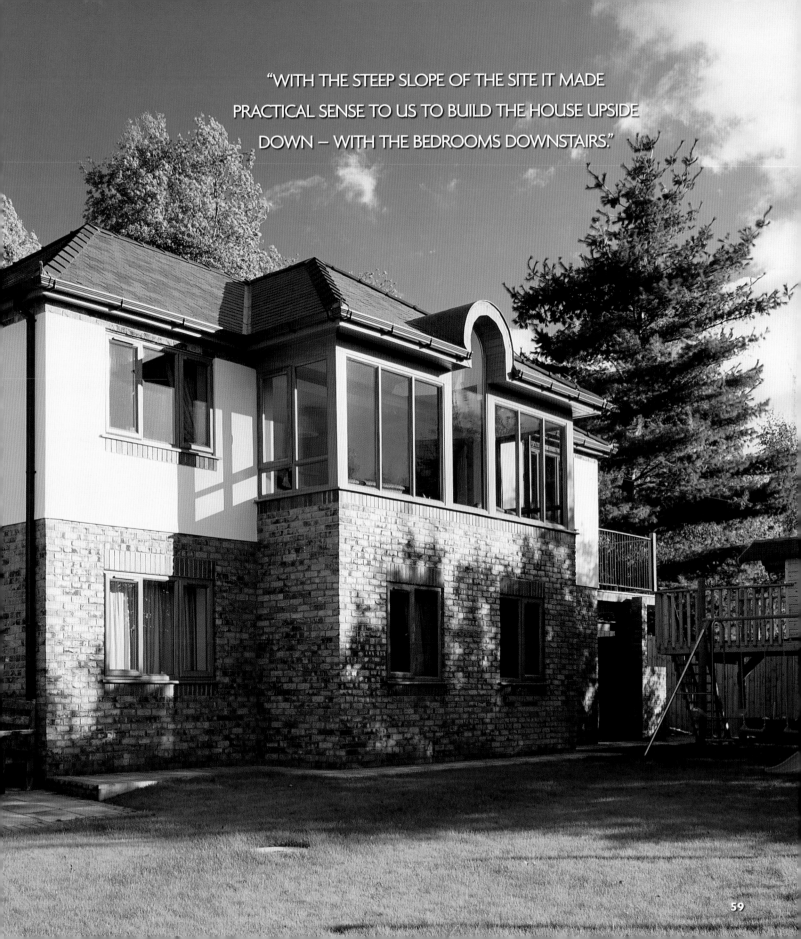

"WITH THE STEEP SLOPE OF THE SITE IT MADE PRACTICAL SENSE TO US TO BUILD THE HOUSE UPSIDE DOWN – WITH THE BEDROOMS DOWNSTAIRS."

 Garry installed the kitchen himself. The furniture and white goods were bought as a package from joinery specialist Howdens for £4,000.

discounted the prospect of having any views from the rear. The site faces south-west, getting direct sunlight on the front elevation in the afternoon. "With the steep slope of the site it made practical sense to us to build the house upside down – with the bedrooms downstairs," says Hayley. "That way we could use our sun lounge and sitting areas to take full advantage of the superb view across the valley – and, of course, the sun setting over the distant hills is fantastic."

With a general idea of the rooms they wanted, and some written ideas to form a brief, they contacted architect Mike Woosnam at the Shearer and Morris practice. He developed their ideas into working layouts for the planning and building regulations applications. The couple allowed what they considered to be plenty of time for building – 18 months to complete and

move in. They both had full-time jobs and a baby son, so were only able to work on the house at weekends and in the evenings during the early stages. "The idea was to build within a tight budget doing as much of the work as I could myself," says Garry. "I can turn my hand to general building – although I did leave the brickwork, plastering and the electrics to specialists."

The whole strategy behind their choice of build method reflected the time they were able to put into it. Although most of the new houses in the area are built using timber frame, the couple opted for brick and block because it allowed them to build at their own pace. The disadvantage was, as winter approached, they realised they were running short of time. They were up to wall plate level but to get the house watertight for the winter, Garry needed to get outside help. "It was comical, really – the one trade I had to get help with was the roofing, which is my speciality!"

By the following August, the finishing line was in sight and they were ready

★ ──────────── UPSIDE DOWN LIVING ──────────── ★

Sloping sites with interesting views offer the perfect opportunity for an innovative designer to 'flip' the layout – with the main day living rooms and kitchen on the first floor and the

bedrooms and utility spaces on the ground floor. This is also an increasingly popular technique in conversion projects where the original building has an interesting roof structure – such as the

beamed ceiling in an old oak barn – that can be used as a design feature for the main living spaces. It also works in tight urban sites where the main source of natural light is from above.

"BUILDING IN MY SPARE TIME WAS QUITE A STRAIN AND PUT US UNDER A LOT OF PRESSURE."

to install the drainage. They'd assumed, and budgeted, for a septic tank – similar to the other houses on the same hillside. The local authority asked them to carry out soil porosity tests – and they were stunned to be told the ground would not be suitable for their proposals. The only alternative, they were told, was to connect to the main sewer a few hundred yards along, and on the other side of the road. The estimate for this was a staggering £20,000.

"It was a devastating blow," recalls Garry. "The prospect of having to find another £20,000 was not a pleasant one." Fortunately, a chance conversation with a nearby neighbour about the drainage issue gave him a glimmer of hope. "The neighbour recommended Waste Tech Sewage Consultants. I contacted them immediately and was really relieved at Maureen Webb's advice. She explained what to do and, following her advice and with relatively little expense, soon had my application for on-site drainage treatment approved. I was able to install it for less than £1,500 – doing most of the work myself, of course."

They moved in during October and took a couple of months to finish up the minor bits and pieces internally. Because of the slope there was no garden to the house – just hillside.

Building a concrete wall would have been incredibly expensive – they knew they couldn't afford it. There are plenty of examples of Gabion baskets in the area, so they decided to investigate. The initial cost from one supplier was over £45 per basket. By contacting the local quarry direct they were able to source the wire baskets for £30 each – and also have the stone delivered to fill them. This was another new trick for Garry to master. "I learned how to fill the baskets, facing up with the better quality stone on the outside – saving myself a lot of money and getting a level garden into the bargain.

"We were building on a budget and Hayley had enough to do looking after our baby son Kieran – she was working too – so we saw very little of each other during the build. That was quite a strain and put us under quite a lot of pressure – but looking back it was worth it to have what we have now.

"It's amazing how the comments have turned around. Now I've lost count of the number of people who say they can't believe we managed to put a house on this site. It just takes some imagination, belief in the potential and quite a bit of time and effort making the idea a reality." ∎

FACT FILE

Names: Garry and Hayley Thomas
Professions: Carpenter and homemaker
Area: Mid Wales
House type: Three-bedroom detached
House size: 147m² + garage
Build route: DIY and directly managed labour
Construction: Masonry and brick
Finance: Private
Build time: April '02-Oct '03
Land cost: £25,000
Build cost: £85,000
Total cost: £110,000
House value: £350,000
Cost/m²: £747 excl. garage

69% COST SAVING

FIRST FLOOR

GROUND FLOOR

FLOORPLAN

The house is built against a steeply sloping hill, so was built on an upside down plan to maximise the light and sense of space in the main living rooms, which have an elevated view across the surrounding valley. The main elevation faces south-west, only getting afternoon sun, the rear is sheltered by the hillside with the ground level built close against the hill. The front entrance door opens onto the hall and landing at first floor, the main living room, kitchen and study open onto it and the stairway leads down to the bedrooms and bathroom.

USEFUL CONTACTS

Designer Mike Woosnam at Shearer & Morris Chartered Surveyors: 01686 625762; **Drainage** Waste Tech **Sewage Consultants** Maureen Webb: 01757 288022; **General building supplies** Boys & Bodens: 01686 626677; **Electrics** Gary Lewis: 01686 624607; **Plumbing supplies** Plumb Center: 01765 690690; **Artexing** Mark Holloway: 01686 670791; **Kitchen units and fittings** Howdens: 01686 610773; **Laminate flooring** B&Q: 01743 448696; **Bricklayers** RD Bennett: 01686 625321; **Gabions** Caerfagu Products: 01597 823087; **Groundworks excavator** Simon Williams: 07977 519554; **PVCu windows and doors** Acorn Frames: 024 7646 6766; **Plasterer** Carl Reynolds: 01686 627613

LYON'S MADE

Malcolm and Jenny Lyon built a home full of light open spaces, which has become a huge financial asset

WORDS: CLIVE FEWINS PHOTOGRAPHY: COLIN BARRATT

MALCOLM LYON BUILT his new timber-framed house for a very specific purpose. "It was to fill a black hole in my life," he says. "I was facing the crisis, aged 60, of premature forced retirement, and I was seeking a rewarding and satisfying 'second career' that would last until my pensions matured."

Malcolm, an engineer by training, and his wife, Jenny, faced five lean years before he was able to draw his pension, so they decided to sink Malcolm's redundancy money and the money from the sale of their house in Bedfordshire into a self-build project in a remote corner of Herefordshire. "The plan was to devise a project that had a good chance of success on a plot that we could buy for a reasonable price, and at the same time produce an asset that would appreciate well in value," Malcolm says.

The main living area, which opens out in to the garden, is dominated by a full-height chimney stack which houses a log-burning stove.

The vaulted roof shows off the internal beams and curved windbraces of the beautiful oak post and beam frame, which add a touch of drama to the double-height living area.

It was a tall order, but Malcolm would modestly admit that they have succeeded on all counts. Although he is now 66 and the project was finished four years ago, the couple are still adding the finishing touches, while at the same time planning on phase two – the conversion of the roof space into two spare bedrooms.

The main build took 18 months in 2002/3. Malcolm and Jenny lived in a rental 10 miles away and the task occupied them both full time for at least six days a week, and often seven, for all that time. "From the outset I wanted to be the main contractor and keep the subbies to the smallest number possible," Malcolm says. "Good project management was a key element of our project, and one of the secrets of that is avoiding over-complication." Because of this there were only three main subcontractors: Welsh Oak Frame, who made and erected the frame and undertook all the footing and the roof; the plumber; and the electricians.

Malcolm himself did most of the joinery, including making the rear oak windows and most of the interior doors, including the oak ones at the south-facing rear of the house, plus the glazed gable end in the upstairs gallery. He also built the magnificent oak staircase – saving an estimated £3,000 in the process.

He and Jenny also designed the house, which is an unusual one-storey ➤

"IT WOULD HAVE BEEN EASY TO HAVE BUILT SOMETHING MORE BASIC AT A LOWER PRICE... AND REGRETTED IT LATER."

Malcolm built
the oak staircase
himself, making a
huge saving.

Malcolm also made the hinged oak doors leading to the kitchen. design with a large gallery that acts as a library and music-listening area. "The design was not easy because of the shape of the site," Malcolm says. "The shape is narrower at the front than at the south-facing rear. It also slopes quite steeply uphill towards the hills and woods that give us such a beautiful view to the rear."

The design they came up with changed several times, but they were keen throughout to use timber frame because they had lived in a Swedish timber-framed house before and liked the feel. As well as this, they also wanted a building that would look right in its setting, and though

modern in its design and interior, would give more than a nod to the local vernacular and not look, as Jenny puts it, "too new."

They, therefore, went for a steeply pitched roof, with reclaimed tiles for the front of the roof and new Chinese slate at the rear. The outer cladding of weatherboarding and brick again reflects local styles.

Getting the design right took a long time, but the planners loved it and it gained approval with absolutely no changes required.

"One of the main challenges was to avoid being penny-pinching," Malcolm says. "We had to be very strict to keep within the budget of £200,000 we had set ourselves, which was to include the purchase of

The gallery overlooks the main living areas and adds valuable floor space.

the plot. At the same time we were greatly concerned about the overall appearance – both inside and out. It would have been easy to have built something more basic at a lower price and then perhaps regretted it later.

"For example, if we had taken a totally hard-headed approach we should have left out the curved windbraces in the roof of the oak-framed section. The engineers said the house would stand perfectly well without them. They are a lovely internal feature, but cost £1,900. However, they add greatly to the aesthetic appeal of the interior and so are a luxury we chose to include."

As well as doing most of the carpentry, Malcolm also did all of ➤

"THE CURVED WINDBRACES IN THE ROOF OF THE OAK-FRAMED SECTION ARE A LOVELY INTERNAL FEATURE, BUT COST £1,900. HOWEVER, THEY ADD GREATLY TO THE AESTHETIC APPEAL OF THE INTERIOR SO WERE A LUXURY WE CHOSE TO INCLUDE."

"THE KITCHEN IS SEPARATED BY TWO FULL-SIZE HINGED OAK DOORS, WHICH CAN BE LEFT OPEN WHEN ENTERTAINING GUESTS."

the plasterboarding, laid the floors, did the external leadwork and (together with Jenny) laid the underfloor heating. Jenny also helped lay the oak floors, decorated the interior and applied all the exterior stains and preservatives.

Despite excellent planning and their own good practical skills, the build still threw up a number of challenges for the Lyons. "We have two types of timber frame: the oak frame at the rear for the main simple three-bay structure, and the softwood frame that houses the entrance and bedrooms, bathrooms and utility rooms," Malcolm explains. "We found that because of the lie of the land, the garage and workshop at the front needed to be built of blockwork because it cuts into the slope and acts as a retaining structure for the rest of the house."

Inside, the main two-storey relaxation area is dominated by the full-height chimney stack that forms a striking central feature. It houses a log-burning stove on the sitting room side. A gallery overlooks the main living areas. "The gallery is a luxury, but we think it adds greatly to the house," says Jenny. Meanwhile, the kitchen is separated by two full-size hinged oak doors, which can be left open when entertaining guests.

"Although we moved in four years ago we feel that managing to do it all for under £200,000, including all the landscaping and driveway, was extremely good. A lot of this was due to a determined drive to be cost-effective, improvising where necessary, seeking the keenest prices, and good project management. And, of course, we made huge savings by doing so much of the work ourselves." ■

FACT FILE

Names: Malcolm and Jenny Lyon
Professions: Retired
Area: Herefordshire
House type: Two/three-bedroom detached
House size: 150m²
Build route: Self-managed
Construction: Masonry at front, timber frame at rear
Warranty: Architect's Certificate
Finance: Sale of previous house plus private
Build time: Oct '01-April '03
Land cost: £65,000
Build cost: £132,000
Total cost: £197,000
House value: £450,000
Cost/m²: £880

54%
COST SAVING

Cost Breakdown:

Oak frame	£19,000	Plumbing	£1,500
Softwood frame	£13,000	Electrics (including connection)	£2,000
Groundworks, foundations and roof (Welsh Oak Frame)	£61,000	Chimney and fireplace	£3,500
		Windows and door frames	£1,300
		Kitchen	£1,500
		Fees and connections	£5,200
		Plastering	£1,300
		Glazing	31,200
		Miscellaneous	£18,000
		TOTAL	**£132,000**

USEFUL CONTACTS

Structural engineer RVW Consulting: 01597 825788 **Oak frame** Welsh Oak Frame: 01686 688000 **Plumbing** Andrew Jukes: 01588 680391 **Electrics** Clun Valley Electrical: 01588 660368 **Chimney system** Anki: 01983 527997 **Kitchen** IKEA: 0845 355 1142 **Sanitaryware** ASE: 01584 873861 **Underfloor heating** Nu-heat: 01404 549770 **Glazing** South Shropshire Glass: 01584 874842 **Windows** Jeld-Wen Premium Range: 0845 122 2890 **Oak** Good Brothers: 01568 708382 **Reclaimed roofing suppliers and general building supplies** John Payne: 01588 660262 **Flooring** Kahrs: 01243 778747 **Bricks** The Brick Library: 01584 879351

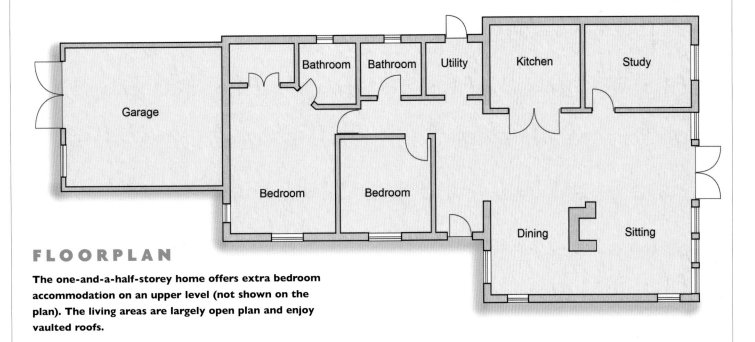

FLOORPLAN

The one-and-a-half-storey home offers extra bedroom accommodation on an upper level (not shown on the plan). The living areas are largely open plan and enjoy vaulted roofs.

Stewart McPherson and
David Richardson have built a
traditional home for just £100,000
on the site of an old cottage they
originally intended to extend.

WORDS: TONY GREENWAY
PHOTOGRAPHY: JEREMY PHILLIPS

It took David Richardson and Stewart McPherson five years to build their dream house. "I had hair when I started this project," smiles David. "But despite all the ups and downs we had during the build, it came good in the end."

David and Stewart's Yorkshire-based home (which includes an on-site boarding cattery business) is a new build, part of which is created in the footprint of a crumbling cottage from the 1700s – and constructed using the cottage's original stone. David and Stewart ➤

OLD STYLE
NEW HOME

have paperwork which dates the cottage to 1786, but there is evidence to suggest it was even older than that. "It was a tithe cottage which had belonged to a large property over the road," explains David. "It had two rooms upstairs and four downstairs, and I'd known about it for years. When I was at school, I'd notice it when I passed on the bus. I'd always liked it."

The house was constructed using stone from the original on-site cottage, and partially built in its footprint. Stewart did all the landscaping work himself.

In 1999, David and Stewart discovered it was to be sold by auction. So, after getting a good price for a previous property, they managed to secure the house and the land – four acres of it in total, including the neighbouring paddock – for £95,000.

"That was seven years ago," says David, "and at the time it seemed like an awful lot of money. We thought we'd rather buy all the land in case a developer snapped up the paddock and got planning permission to build on it. We knew the old cottage was in a terrible state and could see what we were getting from the word go, so we didn't bother to order a survey."

Their plan was to add an extension onto the house and move the bathroom, thus dramatically increasing the space upstairs (to three bedrooms) and downstairs (to six rooms). It wasn't David and Stewart's intention to have to demolish the building and start again.

Securing planning permission had been fraught with problems. "We'd worked with the planners and agreed what we could and couldn't do." says David. "We had the agreed plans drawn up, but after we submitted them we got a letter from our planning officer saying that she couldn't recommend the scheme!" Incompatibility to the local street scene, and complex roof lines were cited in her concerns. ➤

The kitchen was designed to look like an extension. The layout combines well with the rest of the cottage as it sits snuggly at the heart of the home.

The focal point of the lounge is a woodburning fire. The walls have not been plastered 'square' deliberately in order to give the room a rustic feel.

The free-standing bath was from friends of friends, re-enamelled and painted. New England-style tongue-and-groove cladding was installed.

"Thank goodness it wasn't listed!"

Undeterred, David and Stewart submitted their original plans, and prepared for a scheduled site visit to look at the project. Realising they had an opportunity to challenge their planning officer's objections, the pair took photos of all the houses in the immediate area, and made a local pictorial map on a pinboard, and also built a scale model of how the house (featuring the large extension) would look on completion. "None of these measures were permitted in the planning meeting, but we had a captive audience," says David. "It was all out on display in the porch and, after that, it went through easily at the next planning meeting."

Builders were brought in to create the new extension (in October 1999) – but work stopped abruptly when a deep well was uncovered during excavations for the living room foundations. "It had been covered in grass so you couldn't see it was there," remembers David. "It was perfectly lined with red bricks, over five metres deep, and full of rubbish." This was a big problem. The pair's first engineer maintained that the only way to build on such a soft spot would be to pile drive and 'ground beam' the site, potentially costing thousands of pounds. Luckily, David and Stewart's architectural designer brought in his structural engineers. They decided that ➤

"THE COTTAGE WAS IN MUCH WORSE CONDITION THAN ANYONE HAD THOUGHT... THE BUILDERS SAID WE'D BE BETTER OFF PULLING IT DOWN AND STARTING AGAIN."

the problem could be overcome by a conventional, but reinforced, foundation with cantilever.

Unfortunately, as work restarted it became increasingly apparent that the cottage was in much worse condition than anyone had thought: there was no integrity in the stonework and daylight could be seen through big cracks in the walls. "We couldn't knit the structure together," says David. "The builders had a go, but things weren't working out. Underpinning failed, because each hole that was dug caused more damage; so the builders said we'd be better off pulling it down and starting again. I was at work when Stewart gave me a ring to tell me the news. My heart sank because we loved the place, and we didn't buy it to demolish it – it was a little gem."

At that point the budget went out of the window. Originally, £40,000 had been set aside for the extension. David and Stewart were left with

The oak lintel running across the entrance hall was from an old barn. Solid Indian sandstone flags run throughout the downstairs.

two options: they could either put it back on the market and sell what they had, or they could keep going.

On reapplying to the council, further planning consent was given to demolish and rebuild the property, thus rendering it a new build. When it came to pulling the house down, David, his brother Mark, and a family friend, Ken, became the demolition men. "We did it in two-and-a-half days," says David. "We'd already stripped it for the builders to start, so there were no electrics and no plumbing in the shell. We'd also chipped all the plaster off the wall." Sadly, they laid the front of the cottage on the front lawn, stone, by stone, as they worked down. This was to be rebuilt as it was; the stone was 'dressed', and it represented what they loved about the place. "Doing the demolition ourselves meant we could see how desperate the structure really was," says David. "There were beams with barely any 'end bearing' in the walls – quite scary really, but also very sad."

Stewart and David wanted to keep the cottage as previous owners had: honest and simple.

"WE WANTED EVERYTHING HIDDEN, SO WE HAD UNDERFLOOR HEATING RATHER THAN RADIATORS. EXTERNALLY, WE DIDN'T WANT A TV AERIAL ON THE OUTSIDE OR VISIBLE SOIL PIPES."

The builder returned to create the new shell in early 2000, but otherwise, David and Stewart tackled most things themselves. To make the project financially viable, the pair called in a lot of favours, and found some inventive ways to save money. "Apart from using all the original stone and tiles and other salvageable materials for the rebuild," says David, "the log-burning fire in the living room was a present, the flooring was sourced cheaply and the beams we bought were really reasonable: five 15ft oak beams for £50 each. One of these determined the width of the lounge! We had a keen eye for a bargain."

While work was underway in their spare time, the couple stayed with David's family. "I knew the work would get done," says David. "But I don't think we realised just how far we were from the end – because this wasn't a 'price on completion' job, and we were doing bits and pieces as we could afford it. So as soon as a window went in, we'd get really excited! We had the original windows copied and double glazed, and our builder copied the original style of the beamed ceiling for the dining room."

Finally, the house began to take shape and David and Stewart could think about the interior. "We wanted to keep it simple," explains David. "We wanted everything hidden, so we had underfloor heating rather than radiators. Externally, we didn't want a TV aerial on the outside or visible soil pipes. We wanted to keep it as previous owners had: honest and simple."

"We told the plasterer that we didn't want anything 'square'," remembers Stewart. "We said he could leave trowel marks and everything. We wanted the ceilings flat – but that's it. He was horrified by that. Now he loves it, and brings people round to show them the kind of effect rough plastering can give."

When David and Stewart look back, they agree that the worst part of the process was demolishing the original cottage. "Emotionally, that was the worst moment," says David. "Yet things got better – and towards completion, there was a moment when we were eating fish and chips in front of the TV, which was balanced on a barrel in the corner. It was our first meal in the new cottage, and that felt really good. At that point I thought, 'Wow… we're actually getting there.'" ∎

FACT FILE

Names: David Richardson and Stewart McPherson
Professions: Stock controller and cattery owner/manager
Area: Yorkshire
House type: Demolition of original cottage, and then a rebuild with extension
House size: 101m²
Build route: Self-managed with architect and subcontractors
Finance: Savings, shares and sale of former house
Construction: Use of original reclaimed stone and tiles. Oak beams
Warranty: NHBC
Build time: Oct '99-May '03
Land cost: £95,000
Build cost: £100,000

Total cost: £195,000
Current value: £440,000
Cost/m²: £990

56%
COST SAVING

Cost Breakdown:

Flooring	£3,000
Underfloor heating	£2,500
Kitchen	£1,000
Plumbing	£2,500
Electrics	£2,000
Bathroom	£800
Windows and external doors	£4,000
Roof	£3,000
Fees	£2,000
Misc fees, build and labour costs	£79,200
TOTAL	**£100,000**

FIRST FLOOR

GROUND FLOOR

FLOORPLAN

The kitchen is situated in what is designed to look like an extension of the ground floor. The enclosed room layout ties in well with the cottage style exterior.

USEFUL CONTACTS

Builder John Harland: 07931 373933 **Architectural designer** Peter Rayment: 01751 472541 **Plasterer** Jonathan Horne: 01653 618503 **Pine flooring** Penny Bricks of Wetherby: 01937 580580 **Underfloor heating** The Underfloor Heating Company: 01484 860811 **Windows and external doors** S Taylor & Son: 01751 472143 **Wall tiles** Direct Tile Importers: www.directtile.co.uk **Stone flooring** Travis Perkins: www.travisperkins.co.uk **Lighting** Jim Lawrence: 01206 263459

The steep roofpitch means that there is space for a huge playroom in the attic.

COUNTRY MANOR

Serial self-builders John and Katherine Alexander have built a remarkable five times but say their latest project – a spacious country home – is their last.

WORDS: CAROLINE EDNIE   PHOTOGRAPHY: ANDREW LEE

OUR AIM WAS to create a relatively economical but substantial home that would fit in with the country lifestyle of mucky boots and wet jackets. We also wanted a house that was bright and airy and open to the garden." John Alexander is clear about what he and his wife Katherine were looking for from their new home in Lanarkshire. John is also clear that this, the couple's fifth foray into self-building, should be their last.

"We had actually believed that our previous house was our last as we felt settled for a long time. But about two years ago we became unsettled again, so although we had sworn never to build again, we started building our present house in August, and moved in November."

So what lured the couple into committing to Broadwood, their latest self-build, when they were apparently happily domiciled in their previous home?

Although the couple readily admit that they are "compulsive self-builders" at heart, on this occasion their motivation to build was more about the location than the house. "In 1985 we purchased 20 acres of superb woodland grounds in South Lanarkshire that we fell in love with," explains John. Until the self-build bug bit them again and compelled them to build Broadwood, they had built and lived in three houses on the site. "And although our previous house was only 200 yards away, we wanted to build on the site of the former mansion house, which burned down in 1958," says John.

So, did the history of the site have any bearing on John and Katherine's decisions concerning the design of their own 'manor' house? "We put quite a bit of thought into the house," explains John. "We wanted to build a modern home, but with sympathy for the original house. The design reflects the old manor. We wanted a very steep pitch on the roof, crow stepped gables and plenty of narrow windows. We wanted to build a small turret but that was too expensive, although we've got a little balcony like in the original. In no way did we copy the original house, however, because we couldn't have afforded to.

➤

Although the build cost was only £345/m2 the Alexanders were still able to include features like underfloor heating in the conservatory.

"At the same time though, we were also keen to have a nice comfortable family home, which we could finally settle in. In fact it's based to a large extent on the design of our previous house, except that our current house is much bigger. Myself, Katherine and our kids David (17), John (15) and Steven (13), were all involved in the design. We sketched various ideas, and I drew up an original floorplan and elevation. I am a complete amateur when it comes to drawing but I was pleased with how the house turned out in relation to my design. The architects only got involved when we handed them our drawings."

So, how has this combination of modern family comfort, with a splash of baronial stately home, panned out for the Alexanders? "Externally we used a traditional smooth white render, with a very steep 65 degree pitch on the roof. This was finished off with the blonde sandstone crow step gables and heavy matching cills. This was an effective but relatively low cost way of

making the property appear traditional.

"Once inside, there is no pretence of it being an old house – it is just like every modern house, except perhaps in relation to total size. We tried to make rooms generally large enough to be comfortable but not so big that they were difficult to use properly or heat," explains John.

In terms of the internal layout, Broadwood is essentially a two storey, four bedroom house – complete with an amazing football pitch in the attic space. On ground level, as well as an office, music room, kitchen/dining room with sizeable utility space and lounge there is a double height conservatory which the Alexanders admit is one of their favourite features.

"It's not the brightest, sunniest site, but the conservatory gets the light as the sun rises and sets around this part of the building. We wanted the conservatory to look like a modern extension to an old house, which in many ways it does, by means of its full-on glazing effect, double height space, underfloor heating and light pine finishes. The features of the house are practical, not flashy, and throughout the house we have opted for simple paint finishes, standard pine doors and PVCu double glazing. The kitchen is simply MFI, the lighting is from BHS and we pinched the design for our back hall from the farmhouse of our neighbour, so we now have an area where you can kick your muddy boots off."

Upstairs, four en suite bedrooms, with the addition of a family room and games area, complete the picture. "Although the house is not full of stunning features, we have a home that we can honestly say has no faults and there is nothing we would change," claims John. "We did not skimp on the build – we genuinely achieved everything that we had wanted – and by not adding expensive features, we were able to build a larger house. This has resulted in us acheiving a house that is bigger than the areas of the three previous houses that we had built combined. And if we, or any future occupants, want to add stunning features or expensive kitchens and bathrooms, then it can be done easily.

"THE DOUBLE HEIGHT CONSERVATORY IS OUR FAVOURITE ROOM," SAYS JOHN. THE MIX OF CERAMIC FLOOR TILES AND UNDERFLOOR HEATING MAKE THIS ROOM COMFORTABLE THROUGHOUT THE YEAR.

"This is the fifth house we have built, and now for the first time we've got exactly what we want. We learned a lot from the experience of our previous self-builds, but the process of building this house was still not entirely painless," admits John. "Even before the house was built, organising finance proved to be a nightmare. I had done this before and it was incredibly easy; this time, although it was ultimately successful, it was different. In fact I am in the process of cutting my ties with the bank that organised the finance. I felt that they ignored our previous successful self-build projects; furthermore I was inundated with requests for information, including fixed price quotations from bricklayers. I also had to copy every piece of paper, and at times, they were unwilling to accept the terms and conditions that I had agreed with my suppliers," explains John.

"In terms of the actual building process, the biggest problem was when the chap who was supposed to do the drainage and foundation work told me he wasn't going to do it after all – two days prior to starting the job! We had the timber frame kit ordered with the delivery date confirmed, so I ended up having to do it all myself, hiring a machine and laying the concrete foundations as well as laying the drains. In fact the whole family took part in labouring work. I also marked out the site, which I had never done before. But it worked well as I checked it a hundred times – and because we had learned from our previous experience, this time we didn't panic. I should also mention at this stage that John Graham of Cowan Joinery Company, who supplied and erected the kit, was a fantastic help in finding tradesmen and suppliers.

"We would probably not want to go down the self-build route again," concludes John. "We certainly swore not to do so after building this house. Self-build is a rollercoaster – there is a lot of hard work, planning and tough site management to ensure that all trades are on course. Having said this, I think it is quite possible that we would ignore our doubts and convince ourselves to build our retirement home on the basis that it must be easier, because it would probably be less than a quarter of the size of this one." Once compulsive-self builders, always compulsive self-builders, it would seem. ■

FACT FILE

Names: John and Katherine Alexander
Area: South Lanarkshire
House type: Four bed detached
House size: 477m2 + 33m² garage
Build route: Selves as main contractor
Construction: Timber frame with brick cladding
Warranty: Architect's Certificate
Finance: Bank of Scotland
Build time: August '01 – Nov '01
Land cost (est): £85,000
Build cost: £165,000
Total cost: £250,000
House value: £350,000
Cost/m²: £345

29% COST SAVING

Cost Breakdown:

Fees and Admin	£4,161
Foundations	£10,959
Kit and joinery	£64,545
Shell	£11,219
Roof	£5,528
Drains	£2,796
Plumber	£13,691
Plasterer	£6,600
Electrician	£5,776
Flooring	£11,042
Kitchen	£4,870
Bathrooms	£2,363
Tiling	£6,825
Decoration	£2,000
Fireplaces	£4,342
Contingency	£7,836
TOTAL	**£164,557**

FLOORPLAN

The 477m2 house features four bedrooms each with their own en suite bathroom. The steep roofpitch means that there is also a playroom up in the attic.

GROUND FLOOR

FIRST FLOOR

USEFUL CONTACTS

Architects – Sinclair McPhail. 18A Bloomgate, Lanark, ML11 9ET
Structural Engineer – DBM Consultants: 01698 267628;
Construction Frame and Roofing – Cowan Joinery & Construction Co: 01698 884362 (Supplied Nethan Valley Kit) **Builders Merchant** – Buildbase: 01698 351234; **External stonework** – Tradstocks: 01786 850400; **Windows** – Watson Dallas: Tel: 0141 646 2996; **Underfloor Heating and floor tiles** – L&D Ceramics: 0141 643 0602; **Kitchen** – MFI: 01698 540167; **Bath and Shower** – Graham: 01698 841666; **Carpets** – General George: 01698 817135; **Timber flooring** – Hardwood Floors Ltd: 01355 266488
Fireplaces – Welcome Fireplace Co: 0141 429 8242

The vaulted, open plan family room is reminiscent of a converted barn, with flagstone flooring and a flueless stove in the brick fireplace.

SCOTTISH RETREAT

When Michael and Gillian McHugh decided to relocate to the Scottish Borders, Gillian took full responsibility for designing and building their new woodland home.

WORDS: DEBBIE JEFFERY   PHOTOGRAPHY: JEREMY PHILLIPS

ON THE EVE of the new millennium, Michael and Gillian McHugh were celebrating at a party when they made a resolution to drastically change their lifestyle. The following day they purchased a plot of land in a remote village in the Scottish Borders, and started out on their second self-build project in three years and a whole new way of life.

"We were living in Staffordshire with our children, Conor and Megan," explains Gill. "I had built our brick and block house in 1998, which we loved, but it was in a cul-de-sac with five other houses. We wanted to live in rural surroundings, but if we could have picked up our house and transported it to a remote site we would have done so!"

Michael admits to having absolutely no practical skills. In contrast, Gill loves to get her hands dirty, and so she was happy to design the house herself and manage the build. "I was a police officer and had no previous experience of housebuilding," she says.

"We had bought a new estate house when we got married and, after sketching out ideas for extensions and alterations to our existing house, ➤

A self-contained studio apartment above the garage may be used by guests or let out for 'getting away from it all' breaks.

I soon realised that it would be far more economical to build a new property, and went about finding a site and drawing up the plans. I actually prefer to work alone, and Michael is happy to leave everything to me – from hiring the builders to choosing the paint colours."

The couple had tentatively discussed opting out of the rat race for several months, and even considered buying a mobile home and travelling around Europe. They realised that it would be virtually impossible to get back onto the property ladder, however, and instead started searching for a rural site where they could build another house.

"Michael is Scottish, but had no real desire to return there, until we saw an advert on the internet for a one-acre plot with outline planning permission," says Gill. The family jumped into the car on New Year's Day and drove to visit the land near Hawick, armed with a map. What they discovered took their breath away: a tranquil woodland overlooking undulating hills.

The couple immediately decided that they had to buy the land, and Gillian set about designing the perfect house for the setting. The overall layout was

"AS A WOMAN I HAD TO OVERCOME
A CERTAIN AMOUNT OF PREJUDICE
FROM MALE BUILDERS."

based on the McHughs' previous home, although Gill changed the uses of certain rooms. Instead of a playroom there is now a full-height vaulted family room with a breakfast area overlooking the garden.

Once she had completed the design, Gill made what she feels to be a major mistake, and contacted an architect to draw up the plans for the planning application. The architect sited the house on a steep slope in the middle of the plot, which would have required expensive underbuilding. Gillian remained unconvinced, and decided to move the house to a flatter area of ground towards the rear of the plot – which necessitated a new planning application and a four-month delay.

"Using the architect cost about £5,000, and I now realise that I could have managed without one, because most timber frame companies actually redraw your design and liaise with building control on your behalf," Gill explains. "Building control regulations here are stringent, and it took time to gain approval, but we finally got the green light to build in November 2002."

One of Gillian's strengths proved to be her attention to detail. She had researched every aspect of the project prior to work beginning on site so that, by the time the family moved, she had already ordered all the materials – right down to handles and tiles for the bespoke kitchen which she designed herself. This forward thinking ensured that the build went extremely smoothly – taking just seven months from start to finish.

"This build was actually more daunting than the first one," admits Gill. "It's a bit like childbirth. The first time around you have absolutely no idea ➤

In addition to her project management role, Gillian took over some of the subcontracted roles by fixing insulation and laying flooring.

"IT'S A BIT LIKE CHILDBIRTH. THE FIRST TIME AROUND YOU HAVE ABSOLUTELY NO IDEA OF WHAT TO EXPECT. BY THE SECOND TIME YOU ARE FULLY AWARE OF EXACTLY WHAT IS GOING TO HAPPEN!"

Gillian used a traditional style for the family bathroom upstairs.

of what to expect. By the second time you are fully aware of exactly what is going to happen!"

By chance, a small cottage next door to the site was available to rent and, although the McHugh family's belongings ended up scattered between Scotland and Staffordshire, life in the cottage was far better than living in a caravan and meant that Gill could work on site every day.

"We had decided to build in brick and block once again, but discovered that this method of construction did not easily comply with local building regulations for such an exposed location," Gillian explains. "Instead we opted for a timber frame, stuffed with insulation, with roof sarking and slates as stipulated by the planners. After receiving numerous outlandish quotes from timber frame companies we discovered Fouracres Construction Services, who quoted a fantastic price, which included erection, and were helpful and hard working – travelling from Johnston on a daily basis."

Water was brought 1,200 metres across neighbouring fields to the site, which was cleared of some trees and levelled ready for excavation onto bedrock for the foundations. A beam and block floor was constructed and the timber frame erected. The driveway was prepared with 80 tons of hardcore to enable heavy lorries to access the site, but even so, Gillian experienced problems. Due to restricted access, the articulated truck transporting the roof trusses could only get within 1,000 metres of the plot, so Gillian had to hurriedly organise a local farmer with a teleporter

to transport the trusses up the narrow lane, where a crane lowered them into position.

Not content with designing the house and managing the project, Gillian worked alongside the tradesmen in order to learn as much as possible. She spent time driving around building sites to find competent workmen, and then asked if she could watch them as they worked. In this way she has learnt how to do everything from laying underfloor heating to wiring a house.

"As a woman I had to overcome a certain amount of prejudice from the male builders," she admits. "Once they realised that I was serious, however, and saw me getting dirty, fixing insulation, laying flooring and decorating, they had to eat humble pie! Being on site constantly to troubleshoot eliminated the risk of otherwise costly mistakes."

When she is building, Gillian invites a large number of representatives to the site, giving them the opportunity to measure up and explain the benefits of their products. She worked in this way with the roof slaters and window and staircase manufacturers to ensure that, if there were any mistakes with an order, the responsibility for the error rested firmly with the supplier.

"There's a fantastic community spirit here," says Gill, "but it was hard relocating to an area where we knew no one, which gave me the idea to offer my services as a consultant to others hoping to move to the Borders. I am also working as a project manager and self-build advisor, putting all my hard-earned knowledge to good use and doing what I enjoy. We feel very privileged and couldn't be more happy." ■

BUILDING TO A BUDGET

Average building costs in the UK are around £800-1,000/m². Gillian and Michael managed to achieve around two-thirds of this figure thanks to Gillian's hard work on site which reduced labour costs plus her close involvement in managing the project and ensuring a steady flow of labour and materials on site when required.

FACT FILE

Name: Michael and Gillian McHugh
Profession: Project manager, self-build advisor and relocation to the Borders consultant
Area: Scottish Borders
House type: Five-bedroomed detached
House size: 386m² plus garage
Build route: Self-managed subcontractors and DIY
Construction: Timber frame
Warranty: Project Builder – Sterling Hamilton Wright
Finance: Private
Build time: Dec '02-June '03
Land cost: £30,000
Build cost: £215,000
Total cost: £245,000
House value: In excess of £450,000

46%
COST SAVING

Cost/m²: £557
Cost Breakdown:

Professional fees	£10,200
Utilities, wayleave costs	£1,998
Site clearance	£6,040
Foundations	£5,076
Mains water, drainage, septic tank	£8,170
Insurances and warranty	£1,813
Labour and materials	£182,392
TOTAL	**£215,392**

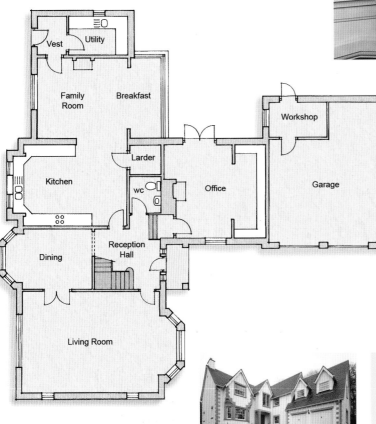

FLOORPLAN

Gillian based the floorplan on the layout of the family's previous house, including a vaulted family room and conservatory style breakfast room in place of the playroom. There is a separate, formal dining room, and a ground floor study with its own library area for Michael, with a guest suite above the garage suitable for holiday lets.

"BEING ON SITE CONSTANTLY TO TROUBLESHOOT ELIMINATED THE RISK OF OTHERWISE COSTLY MISTAKES."

USEFUL CONTACTS

Designer and project manager Gillian Murphy-McHugh: 01450 880332, gillianmmchugh@aol.com; **Kitchen units** Moorland Pine Centre: 01538 387799; **Timber frame** Fouracres Construction Services: 01505 337788; **Plasterer** Gavin Brodie: 01450 870027; **Joiner** Dave Noble: 01968 661588; **Roofing** SI Roofing: 01324 876363; **Windows** Roxburghe Windows: 01450 378655; **Electrician** Alan Smith: 01450 371124; **Plant hire and driver** Mitchell Stenhouse: 01450 372865; **Underfloor heating** Borders Underfloor Heating: 01361 850637; **Flagstones** Classical Flagstones: 0117 937 1960; **Fireplaces** Warmsworth Stone: 01302 858617; **Flueless fires** Burley Appliances Ltd: 01572 756956

FABULOUS IN FLINT

First-time self-builders Rory and Hayley Joseph built their traditional four-bedroomed detached home on a tight plot and an even tighter budget.

WORDS: DEBBIE JEFFERY PHOTOGRAPHY: ROB JUDGES

WHEN WE FIRST found a plot of land and started to think about building our own house, we were very naïve – particularly about what it might cost," admits Rory Joseph. "We set a provisional budget of £80,000 but soon realised that we'd been totally unrealistic. Now that we understand exactly what is involved in a self-build, we know that our actual budget of £120,000 was an excellent price for building a four-bedroomed detached house."

Rory was first inspired to self-build after reading a copy of Homebuilding & Renovating magazine at work. "I was a mortgage advisor for an estate agent and we were marketing a house which had featured in the magazine," he explains. "Everyone in the office read the article, but for me it was the catalyst which planted the idea of building a house firmly in my mind."

After a long search for a suitable building plot, the couple got lucky and found a piece of land on the edge of a new development near Newmarket. ➤

"I DID GUESS A LOT OF THE FIGURES AND FORGOT ABOUT SOME BASIC THINGS – LIKE NEEDING HOT WATER."

A farmer had sold off a package of land, where seven large properties had been constructed, but had retained the end site. It was this extremely compact plot, with planning permission for a new dwelling, which the Josephs purchased for £100,000 and also came with a derelict Victorian barn which they planned to convert into a garage with a useful studio room above.

"We approached Potton to design us a timber-framed house because we had seen their brochures and liked the idea of an experienced company who would hold our hand throughout the build," says Rory. He and Hayley chose to modify the Elmdon from Potton's Shire range of traditional-style homes, changing the interior layout to suit their needs and adapting the exterior shape until the planners were eventually satisfied. Panels of flintwork were specified in order that the new property would fit in with the neighbouring houses and sit comfortably within the existing brick and flint wall which encircles the site.

After a year-long delay while their detailed planning application was considered – during which time the couple had their first baby, Maya – the build itself proved to be incredibly straightforward. Hayley made progress charts to help organise the process and everything seemed to be going swimmingly until one of the neighbours complained about the ridge height – just as the roof tiling was finally completed. Retrospective planning was then required for the marginally higher ridge height, and the application had to go before a full planning committee – which proved extremely traumatic for the Josephs, who waited with baited breath to discover whether they would need to take down their roof and rebuild it using new roof trusses.

"By this stage we were desperate to move in because we were paying rent and a mortgage on the new house," says Hayley. "Luckily the retrospective planning application was accepted and we handed in notice on our rented accommodation in the spirit of great optimism, expecting to move straight into our new home. What we didn't realise is that, while building a house doesn't seem to take that long, the finishing takes much longer and is terribly expensive – far more than we had budgeted."

Terracotta floor tiles were chosen for the traditional kitchen, with hand-painted pine units (which Hayley and Rory fitted themselves), beech worktops and a range cooker. ➤

Chestnut flooring has been laid in the sitting room, where the large brick fireplace incorporates a reclaimed bressumer beam.

Rory takes full responsibility for the overspend. "I'm ashamed to say that I did guess a lot of the figures and forgot about some basic things – like needing hot water, which meant that we couldn't afford to have underfloor heating throughout the whole house as we had originally planned," he admits. Despite their rather haphazard budgeting, the Josephs still managed to build the house for a relatively modest £120,000, and did not stint when it came to choosing high-quality building materials.

In addition to the panels of decorative external flintwork favoured by the Parish Council, they also chose clay roof tiles and timber windows. "We saved some money by convincing the planners to allow us to use ready-made flint blocks," says Hayley. "These are extremely heavy, though, so instead of using Rendalath externally we had to clad the entire house in a skin of solid blockwork which would support the weight."

Internally, the Josephs continued to specify the best that they could afford, shopping carefully and choosing to upgrade items such as the wooden

WE WANTED TO MAKE SURE THAT WE WOULDN'T FEEL AS THOUGH WE WERE LIVING IN COLDITZ, SO WE DESIGNED A HIGH BRICK AND FLINT TERRACE WHICH TURNED OUT TO BE A REAL SUNTRAP."

Tumbled slate tiles form splashbacks in the main bathroom which features a traditional roll-top bath.

doors, staircase and skirting boards – which all came as part of the Potton package. Electric underfloor heating was fitted in the kitchen, utility and dining room to one side of the hallway, with standard radiators in the remaining rooms. The sitting room features a large brick fireplace, with a heavy bressumer beam sourced from a reclamation yard, and their solid pine kitchen units have been hand-painted and fitted with beech worktops for a classic feel. Hayley and Rory saved money by tackling as much of the work as possible and laid all of the chestnut flooring themselves, as well as fitting the kitchen, tiling and decorating.

"We moved into the house when Maya was six months old and before the electricity was connected, so for the first two weeks we used candles and heated her bottles using a diesel generator," recalls Rory. "It took another couple of months to finish off the interiors and complete the landscaping. The house has been built quite low down on the site, but with such a high boundary wall already in place, we wanted to make sure that we wouldn't feel as though we were living in Colditz, so we designed a relatively high brick and flint terrace, stepped up from the main house, which turned out to be a real suntrap.

"We would love to build again, although finding a plot is definitely the hardest part," Rory explains. "Obviously we have learnt a huge amount from the project and would certainly know how to budget better in the future, but the house has been valued at £365,000 which means that we managed to save 40% by building for ourselves, so I don't think we did too badly." ■

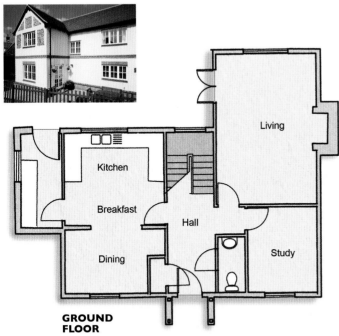

GROUND FLOOR

FIRST FLOOR

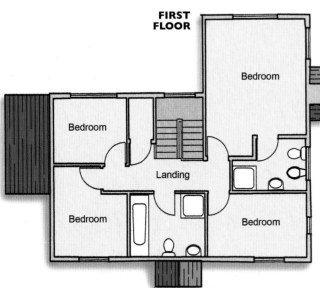

FLOORPLAN

The kitchen is open plan to the dining room and has a separate utility room. To the other side of the hallway there is a study, cloakroom and a lounge, whilst upstairs three bedrooms share the family bathroom and the master bedroom has a private en-suite.

FACT FILE

Names: Rory and Hayley Joseph
Professions: Director of mortgage brokerage and homemaker
Area: Cambridgeshire
House type: Four-bedroomed detached
House size: 145m²
Build route: Timber frame kit, subcontractors and DIY
Finance: Skipton Building Society
Construction: Timber frame, blockwork, flint blocks, clay roof tiles
Warranty: Zurich
Build time: Jan '03-Aug '03
Land cost: £100,000
Build cost: £120,000
Total cost: £220,000
Current value: £365,000
Cost/m²: £828

40%
COST SAVING

Cost Breakdown:

Potton kit	£30,130
Flint blocks	£1,053
Roofing slates	£952
Bricks	£1,905
Blocks	£1,783
Kitchen and utility cupboards	£2,535
Floor and wall tiles	£1,592
Beech worktops	£395
Wood flooring	£1,742
Underfloor heating mat	£320
Sanitaryware, taps, towel radiator	£3,350
Fireplace beam	£162
Patio slabs	£1,058
Softwood doors	£150
Paint, stain and varnish	£773
Materials (timber, sand, cement etc.)	£14,500
Labour	£58,000
TOTAL	**£120,400**

USEFUL CONTACTS

Timber frame Potton Ltd: 01767 676400 **Kitchen** Pineland Furniture Ltd: 01299 271143 **Building materials** B&Q: 0845 222 1000 **Kitchen tiles** Fired Earth: 0845 366 0400 **Bathroom tiles** Topps Tiles: 0800 783 6262 **Materials** Homebase: 0870 900 8098 **Wood flooring** Petersons Natural Floorings: 01603 755511 **Terracotta floor tiles** York Handmade Brick Co: 01347 838881 **Shower trays** City Plumbing Supplies Holdings plc: 01633 265365 **Paint** Focus (DIY) Ltd: 0800 436436 **Reclaimed fireplace beam** Solopark plc: 01223 834663 **Building materials** Ridgeons Ltd: 01223 466000 **Flint blocks** Dorset Flint & Stone Blocks: 01258 880030 **Fixtures and fittings** Screwfix Direct: 0500 414141 **Bath** Bathroom Discount Centre: 020 7381 4222 **Roof slates** Stone & Slate Ltd: 01246 250088 **Sanitaryware** Wickes: 020 8901 2000

AN OAK COTTAGE FOR £48K

With the help of family and friends, Paul and Jo Suter have built a three-bedroomed oak-framed cottage for a total cost of under £100,000.

WORDS: DEBBIE JEFFERY PHOTOGRAPHY: COLIN BARRATT

FOR TWO YEARS Jo and I were technically homeless while we tried to find a plot of land to buy," explains Paul Suter. "We had sold our small cottage, which we thought put us in a good position to move quickly when something came up. Unfortunately, we missed out on every plot we tried to buy, and while we waited land prices were escalating. We spent time living with my parents, then moved in with Jo's parents, then went back to mine for another few months to try to avoid outstaying our welcome. We were growing increasingly worried and began to look at houses instead of land, because we felt that building was just beyond our means."

A plasterer by profession, Paul knew a number of people who had built their own homes and saved money in the process. With a total budget of just £100,000 he and Jo hoped that self-build would offer a way back onto the housing ladder, but were determined not to overspend.

"We managed to save a bit of money while we were living rent-free with our parents," says Jo, "but we soon realised that land and property prices were soaring and we were running out of time. What we wanted was to build a home that we could enjoy, without over-stretching ➤

ourselves financially. There would be no point completing something that we couldn't afford to furnish or live in."

Paul's brother works for the Herefordshire based company Border Oak, which designs and builds green oak framed buildings, and Paul decided to approach the company's founder, John Green, for advice regarding his budget. "I went to see him with my figures, and knew he would be honest," Paul recalls. "John told me that it would be possible to build something — at a push. I didn't think for one second that we could afford to build an oak-framed house."

After yet another failed attempt to buy a plot at auction, Paul and Jo received a telephone call from John Green telling them about some building land he had bought in Yarpole where he hoped to build two oak framed cottages. The Suters went to see the plot, which they loved, and discussed a design for a simple three-bedroomed cottage with John.

Although there was already a 1930s prefab on the site, gaining planning permission for two new dwellings proved quite difficult. Paul and Jo wrote a letter to the planners explaining that they were a young local couple who wanted to build their own home and start a family, but could not

The brick fireplace in the sitting room was built by Paul's father and fitted with a woodburning stove.

find an affordable plot in the area.

"The land had cost us £49,000, so we had just £51,000 remaining," says Jo, an insurance clerk. "Paul's dad is a builder, who very kindly gave up work for several months to help us with the build, and our friends also lent a hand — which meant that we were able to tackle around 90 per cent of the building work ourselves and saved a great deal of money. I was working and Paul had just started up his own dry-lining company, but his father worked on site seven days a week — we owe him a great deal."

Situated on the edge of the village, the couple's mature garden plot already had an apple tree, shrubs and hedges, which they managed to retain during the build. Paul's father, Roy, prepared the foundations and slab, building up the ground floor external walls in cavity brick and blockwork ready for Border Oak to erect the first floor oak frame and rendered infill panels. The chimney has been constructed on the front elevation to enable French windows in the gable end to open onto the south facing rear garden.

"JOHN TOLD ME THAT IT WOULD BE POSSIBLE TO BUILD SOMETHING — AT A PUSH. I DIDN'T THINK FOR ONE SECOND THAT WE COULD AFFORD TO BUILD AN OAK-FRAMED HOUSE."

Beautifying on a budget: MFI units and beech worktops have been fitted in the kitchen, which is set off with a natural slate floor and chrome accessories.

Making the most of the available space, a nursery has been built above the garage.

Paul and Jo spent every spare moment working on site, and Paul helped his father tile the roof and completed all of the internal plastering. "When I mentioned to Dad that I'd had a quote for £2,000 to tile the roof he told me that we could do it ourselves," says Paul. "We used reclaimed clay tiles which meant there was about 20 per cent wastage, and each one needed to be carefully checked for frost damage or cracks, but the end result looks lovely."

Jo is afraid of heights, which meant that she could not climb the scaffolding or go upstairs in the cottage until the staircase was installed, and had not seen the views from the bedroom windows across open fields beyond the garden. Instead, she worked on the ground, loading bricks and labouring.

Paul spent three days making the internal ledge and brace doors, saving several hundred pounds. All the remaining joinery, including the windows and staircase, was constructed by a local company in idigbo hardwood, which looks similar to oak.

"We spent a fortune on self-build books and magazines, and would have loved to buy some of the luxury fixtures and fittings we saw advertised," says Jo. "We stuck to our guns though and ordered an MFI kitchen, which we dressed up with chrome accessories, stonewashed marble splashbacks and slate flooring."

While they were in the shop, Paul spotted some handmade white tiles with raised frog motifs, which he decided to buy for the bathroom. He had fixed them to the wall and was about to start to grout when he heard Jo crying because she hated them so much. In a rage Paul hacked the tiles off the walls and broke them up with a jackhammer, wasting £170 in the process. Just one was saved and fixed behind the door, where Jo did not even notice it until three weeks later!

"Most of our building materials came from Jewson," says Paul. "I know that people tend to try and knock down prices by playing suppliers off against one another, but I think that this can waste time and it can annoy them. I did occasionally suck my teeth to try and get them to drop a price, but overall they were very good.

"We love it here, and never envisaged moving – although we are now starting to talk about building again! It has been such a fantastic experience and, at £48,000, we actually came in under budget thanks to all the help from family and friends. We can't thank them enough." ■

FACT FILE

Names: Paul and Jo Suter
Profession: Plasterer and insurance clerk
Area: Herefordshire
House type: Three-bedroomed detached cottage
House size: 110m²
Build route: DIY
Construction: Brick and block ground floor, oak-framed first floor; clay roof tiles
Warranty: Architect's Certificate
Finance: Britannia stage payment mortgage
Build time: April '01-May '02
Land cost: £49,000
Build cost: £48,000
Total cost: £97,000
House value: £310,000
Cost/m²: £436

69%
COST SAVING

Cost Breakdown:

Planning, fees and utilities	£3,500
Foundations and slab	£3,000
Ground floor and chimney	£5,000
Oak frame	£8,500
Roof and clay tiles	£4,300
External joinery	£3,500
First and second-fix joinery, incl. kitchen	£8,500
Plumbing and electrics	£7,000
Landscaping	£2,000
Miscellaneous	£2,800
TOTAL	**£48,100**

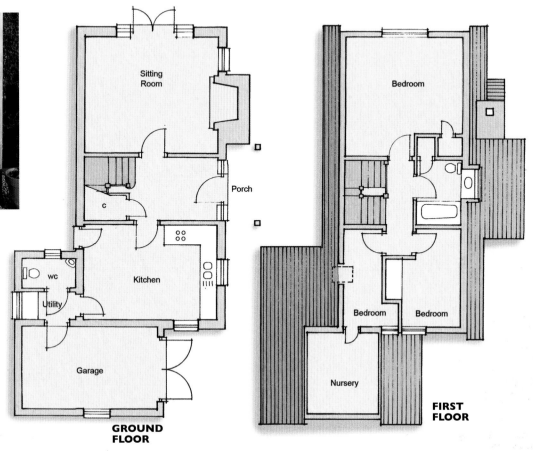

GROUND FLOOR

FIRST FLOOR

FLOORPLAN

The cottage has a simple two bay layout with a central hallway leading into the sitting room on one side and the kitchen, WC and utility to the other. Upstairs there are three bedrooms and a bathroom, with a playroom constructed above the weatherboarded garage.

USEFUL CONTACTS

Design and oak frame Border Oak: 01568 708752; **Woodburner** Clearview Stoves: 01584 878100; **Softwood joinery and weatherboarding** Pontrilas Timber: 01981 240444; **External doors and windows** Hamwyn Joinery: 01568 797650; **Clay roof tiles and calculations** Thomas Smith Roofing: 01432 273084; **Dry-lining** Paul Suter Drylining Ltd: 07702 220709; **Slate floor and wall tiles** County Tiles, Ludlow: 01584 879786; **Kitchen** – MFI: 0800 192192; **Building materials** Jewson: 02476 438400; **Sanitaryware** Bathroom Express: 01633 244555

BUILDING A KIT HOUSE ★ £120,000

POLISH PREFAB

WORDS: DEBBIE JEFFERY   PHOTOGRAPHY: COLIN BARRATT

Derek and Natasha Marshall's impressive new 'kit' house was completed in just 11 weeks and cost £120,000 to build.

SITUATED IN A small village in the Scottish Borders, the unusual design of the Marshalls' house is all the more distinctive due to its location in a residential neighbourhood that dates back to the 1960s. This Dan-Wood house (the Polish equivalent of the prefabricated German-built Huf House) is the first of its kind to be built in the UK. That it is here at all is down to architect Derek Marshall having the courage of his convictions – even when asked to pay a hefty deposit for something he hadn't seen.

This remarkable story began in 2002 when Derek and his Ukrainian wife, Natasha, both divorcees, met through the internet. Romance blossomed and it wasn't long before Natasha decided to give up her home and radio manager's job in the Ukraine and create a new life with Derek in Scotland.

"As we were both starting again, we wanted to build from scratch," says Derek. In August 2003, the couple purchased a small plot (12.5 metres × 22 metres) in a picturesque village with views of the nearby Eildon Hills.

Derek came up with a detached two-storey house design to suit the plot's narrow 12.5 metre frontage and had just submitted it for planning approval when he heard of a move to introduce highly insulated quick-to-build (six weeks is the norm) prefabricated houses to the UK from Poland. "Unfortunately there was nothing in the UK for us to see," explains Derek, "but the all-inclusive price was good, the company has an excellent and long-established track record in Europe, and the specification – on paper at any rate – appeared vastly superior to anything available here."

Negotiations were complicated as no one at Dan-Wood spoke good ➤

The Marshalls' house features a sloping roof that extends to form a double carport. The distinctive cladding is a shade of green called Seclusion — a colour Derek and Natasha liked so much they named their house after it.

The master bedroom features rooflights which not only make it a light and airy space, but which also give stunning views.

English. Natasha solved the problem by stepping in and communicating with them in Russian.

Dan-Wood's timber frame houses are prefabricated in the factory in Poland, their huge closed-cell panels incorporating everything from service conduits to the finished external wall render on one side, and pre-decorated plasterboard on the other. "The downside is that you have to make decisions right at the very beginning regarding the position of electrical sockets, light switches and the like," says Derek.

But the specification was impressive. "Scottish kit houses use lightweight timbers, whereas the Polish use much heavier timbers. The outside frame consists of 180mm x 50mm studs with 12.5mm OSB board on both sides. Most of the internal partitions are 150mm x 50mm studs with the same board both sides – twice as thick as the normal UK specification, which on a practical level makes it easier to put up shelves and so on."

Despite being asked to pay 40 per cent of the cost upfront, the couple decided to go ahead and Derek sent his drawings off to Poland. This large pre-payment has now been reduced to a more acceptable five per cent deposit and all Dan-Wood's supply-and-erect costs are exempt from VAT.

The upstairs sitting room/study can be partially divided by storage units to turn the top half into a guest room if required.

The Dan-Wood system depends on the customer putting in a concrete base slab and bringing in the services. That part complete, the Marshalls' house was delivered on the back of three articulated lorries. "They were lined up in a nearby lay-by," recalls Derek. "One by one they unloaded and moved off. It was amazing to watch. Everything is on these lorries, from the pre-decorated wall panels and concrete roof tiles, to paints, finishes, door ironmongery, solid oak flooring and reserve supplies – all neatly packed in protective waterproof material. The only items not included were the kitchen units and appliances, because of the extensive choice available."

Work started on Monday, September 5, when a crane began lowering the panels into position. Says Derek: "We had to close the top of the road off to traffic during the day, but within three hours you could walk on the first floor, by the second night the house was watertight – and on Friday we had a wine and whisky tasting evening for the Polish workforce.

"The only wet process in the house is the concrete floor screed – 80mm rigid insulation board topped by a 40mm self-levelling gypsum floor screed. The same base is laid on the first floor, which provides superb sound insulation, although the floor joists have to be thicker to support the extra weight."

Derek managed the project himself but quickly discovered the workforce was so skilled he had very little to do other than stand back and watch in amazement as the house went up around him. "In our case a team of five multi-skilled Polish workers arrived with the house and saw the build through from start to completion," says Derek. "They were brilliant – non-smokers, polite, friendly, and they worked six days a week. The screed, ➤

"THEY WERE ALL LINED UP IN A NEARBY LAY-BY. ONE BY ONE THEY UNLOADED AND MOVED OFF. IT WAS QUITE AMAZING TO WATCH."

The emphasis on natural materials and practical surfaces continues in the entrance hall, which has slate-effect floor tiles and an ash open tread staircase.

The kitchen features olive-coloured wall and base units with a wood-grain effect and long slimline stainless steel handles, their clean lines echoed by a flat ceramic hob and sleek overhead chimney extractor.

"A TEAM OF FIVE MULTI-SKILLED POLISH WORKERS ARRIVED WITH THE HOUSE AND SAW THE BUILD THROUGH FROM START TO COMPLETION."

which usually takes three or four weeks to dry out, took an extra week – during which time the workers helped with the decking outside."

Everything went smoothly from day one. "Polish plumbers came over to do the first fix, while the team that was here did the second fix as well as everything else," says Derek. Not only does this save time and hassle having to source and liaise with individual tradesmen — something most self-builders in the UK have to contend with — it also results in less mess, given that the workmen who prepare the walls will also be painting them later, so they tend to take greater care and clean up as they go.

Apart from the design, which in this instance was Derek's, everything in the Marshalls' house is standard, even the wooden pull-down loft ladder. The German STO render system is applied in the factory as standard, leaving only the final coat to be applied on site; the thermal-efficient double glazed full-height windows on the ground floor and the tilt and turn

windows elsewhere have timber surrounds, which, like the internal woodwork, have a PVCu-like lacquered finish; and in addition to a choice of sanitaryware and tiling, the couple also opted for a standard ash open-tread staircase and balustrade.

The Polish workers left six weeks to the day they arrived, and when Derek and Natasha moved in seven days later, the house was totally finished, painted and decorated. Apart from minimum shrinkage, they haven't had any problems.

"Not only is it a very pleasant house to live in, it's also very economical," says Derek. "Owing to the high insulation, the central heating radiators can be smaller — and are always at a low setting." A quirky feature that's also standard in Dan-Wood houses is an upstairs cupboard that provides access to a heating manifold, allowing individual radiators to be turned off at source. As the loft will only ever be used for storage, the house has a 'cold roof' — the insulation is at ceiling level.

Although a newcomer to the UK, Dan-Wood houses are fully mortgageable and the company provides a 30-year structural guarantee. Dan-Wood is currently negotiating with Zurich to provide a ten-year construction guarantee.

Derek has been so impressed by the whole experience he now has a Dan-Wood agency and is actively promoting the company's property portfolio in Scotland and the North of England. "The average price of a Dan-Wood house is around £650-£700 per square metre, which compares very favourably with UK prices. In every other respect it's way ahead. The system is efficient, everything arrives on schedule, the workforce gets on with the job virtually unaided, and six weeks later the house is finished. How many self-builders in the UK can say that?" ∎

PACKAGE HOMES

An increasing number of self-builders such as Derek and Natasha are opting for 'turnkey' approaches, whereby the design and construction (materials and labour) of their new home is entirely outsourced to a design/build company. The vast majority of these companies operate in the timber frame sector and many, such as Dan-Wood, specialise in closed-panel, prefabricated systems, whereby fully finished wall panels can be delivered in one go to site and erected by a team of imported labour. This massively reduces time on site, although there is, of course, a significant lead-in time of up to three months.

FLOORPLAN

The 140m² home contains an open plan arrangement downstairs, with two bedrooms upstairs.

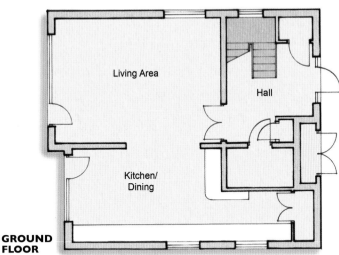

GROUND FLOOR

THE POLISH WORKERS LEFT SIX WEEKS TO THE DAY THEY ARRIVED, AND WHEN DEREK AND NATASHA MOVED IN SEVEN DAYS LATER, THE HOUSE WAS TOTALLY FINISHED.

FACT FILE

Names: Derek and Natasha Marshall
Professions: Architect and project manager
Area: Scottish Borders
House type: Detached two-bedroom house
House size: 140m²
Build route: Self-managed with sub-contractors
Construction: Concrete base slab and Dan-Wood timber frame
Finance: Private and mortgage
Build time: 11 weeks, from August to October 2004
Land cost: £47,000
Build cost: £120,500
Total cost: £167,500
House value: £215,000
cost/m²: £861

71%
COST SAVING

Cost Breakdown:

Foundations, services and floor slab	£14,000
Dan-Wood turnkey house	£95,500
Kitchen units and fitting	£2,500
Plant hire, site storage and skips	£3,000
Paths, paving, fencing and decking	£5,500
TOTAL	**£120,500**

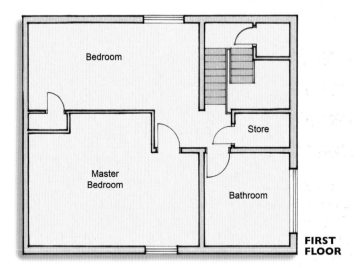

FIRST FLOOR

USEFUL CONTACTS

Architect Derek Marshall RIBA: 01896 753077 **Timber frame** Dan-Wood Concept Plus: 01896 752271 **Ground works** Craigvar Construction: 01896 752828 **Fencing** First for Fencing: 01896 823717 **Scaffolding** John Laidlaw & Sons Ltd: 01835 862524 **Tiles** Edinburgh Tile: 01896 757577 **Blinds** Athena Blinds: 01968 678792 **Kitchen works and bathroom furniture** Buildbase Ltd: 01236 454454

PROVING THEM WRONG

Velma and Kevin Skingsley have built a large family home for just £115,000.

WORDS: DAVID SNELL   PHOTOGRAPHY: ANDREW PRIEST

"HELLO DAVID. I hope that you are well. I was just going through some of my folders and I came across the letter you wrote to me telling me I had 'ideas above my station in life', when I'd told you that I was planning to build a six-bedroomed house. Well, I have just finished and I'm hoping that you can come and see it very soon."

That's the gist of the letter I got a little while ago from Velma Skingsley (née Scott). Of course, she knew that I was joking and, in any event, like so many of those who take part in Plotfinder Challenge, we had been in touch quite a few times and I was only really waiting for her to tell me that she had finished before going up to see her.

When we did the challenge in 2002 I'd been impressed with Velma's determination to self-build. Kevin, her then partner, now husband, and their two children tried to involve themselves in her passion but they could never hope to share it fully. She made it happen – although she's quick to point out, she couldn't/wouldn't have done it without their support.

They didn't get the plot she chose from the ➤

Velma and Kevin had their hearts set on natural materials for the exterior – they bought the natural stone for just £27/m².

Light comes into the living room through a large bay window – PVCu was chosen when the timber window company failed to turn up.

challenge: a spare piece of land owned by the electricity board which had been on the market for ages at £40,000. Velma's diary records her absolute despair at losing the plot, but she came home that night and went onto the internet. There were two plots in Chesterfield on a road she had always wanted to live in.

"I used to live in a one-bedroomed council flat at the top of the hill and had to walk down to this road to catch the bus to work. I said to myself then, 'one day I'll live on this road,' and now I do."

The plots were for sale at £25,000 each, but Velma had no intention of building two houses. She put in an offer of £47,000 without telling Kevin – and then the agents came back to say that the vendor wanted to meet them, so she had to tell him what she'd done. Luckily Kevin was keen and they went along with every intention of winning the plots. "It was like he wanted to interview us," Velma recalls, "Which is fair enough I suppose, as

"I'VE BUILT A SIX-BEDROOM, THREE-STOREY HOUSE IN NATURAL STONE WITH A SLATE ROOF FOR £115,000."

we were his prospective neighbours. The following day we got a call to say that if we upped our offer to the full asking price it was ours."

A quick check with the planners that they were OK with one instead of two houses and Velma and Kevin found themselves the prospective owners of the plot, with their home on the market. One week later the house was sold and they began to make arrangements to move into rented accommodation.

And that's when it all came to a grinding halt. There was a covenant on the land whereby the vendor had to pay a percentage of any uplift to the local authority. He was quite prepared to do so but the legalities dragged on. "Still, I wasn't going to waste the time," says Velma. "First of all I had to get the planning. I went to see an architect but he wanted so much money and when I told him I was going to project manage, he sort of scoffed. So I sent off for various brochures and houseplan books and we came up with our own ideas for a three-storey house. Then I got a local chap to draw it up for me.

"We put it in for planning, but then the neighbours objected. However, we got it in the end; along with Building Regulations approval. So there we were, all ready to go and yet I didn't own the plot. It was a full year before it was mine."

It must have been galling but it is perhaps one reason for the amazing success of this self-build. Velma tells me that builders' merchants and ➤

The light, open feel of the house continues through into the kitchen/dining room.

The master bedroom is one of six, and features built-in wardrobes for a clutter-free finish.

"I USED TO LIVE IN A COUNCIL FLAT AT THE TOP OF THE HILL AND HAD TO WALK DOWN THIS ROAD TO CATCH THE BUS . I SAID TO MYSELF, 'ONE DAY I'LL LIVE ON THIS ROAD', AND NOW I DO."

suppliers contacted her and asked if they could quote – but she is a great negotiator and she screwed them right down; she played every trick in the book and got prices that many a seasoned developer would envy. The same with the labour. She and Kevin had an extension at their previous home and they'd lined the builders up to do the new house on a labour-only basis. It was going to be built of stone. At first Velma was thinking in terms of reconstituted stone but Kevin felt that they should use natural. Velma baulked at the price but then negotiated a deal to buy dressed Matlock stone for just £27/m².

"Once the land was ours I rang the builders to tell them they could start, only to be told by the son that his dad had suffered a heart attack and they couldn't do it," Velma relates. "Up until then everything had been based on them doing the superstructure. We needed some natural stone for the dry stone walls at the front and, eventually, more at the back. Kevin found a farmer who had some for sale and we bought it for

£600, and he introduced us to some guys who did the foundations."

Work started – but shortly afterwards had to stop as, despite Transco telling them the site was clear, a gas pipe was discovered running just behind the rear trenches. It took six weeks for them to deal with it and, when they did, it took a few minutes to fix in a short length and simply push it to the side of the excavation.

Velma had used the time to find builders for the superstructure. "I got quotes and then another builder contacted me. I wasn't that interested at first but went to see his work and I thought, 'I like him. He's the kind of guy that could sit around our dinner table,' so we did a deal. In the end he was great."

By August, five months after starting, the roof was on and the scaffolding ready to be taken down. "We found that the scaffolding company had gone bust," Velma reports, "Nobody would touch it. In the end the guy who owned the firm came and dropped it and we paid him a cheque

The house features simple timber finishes for a classic appeal. Both interior and exterior doors are glazed to bring in maximum light.

made out to the bankrupt company."

The timber window company took forever to come and in the end Velma and Kevin opted for a local PVCu window company, which enabled the plasterer to finish by the end of September. The plumber was a disaster – though he was CORGI registered, with all the necessary qualifications. "I got to site one time," Velma remembers, "and there were some boys doing the job. I asked where the plumber was and they said he'd gone off to get something. I told them to stop and when he did turn up I told him I wanted the job done by a professional."

All these problems added to Velma's experience and will stand her in good stead when she does it again – "As I will," she tells me. "I've already got a plot in mind and we're hoping to renovate. Everybody told me I was mad: my friends, my family, builders, architects. But I've proved them wrong. I've built a six-bedroom, 267m², three-storey house in natural stone with a slate roof for £115,500. The total costs with land are £165,500 and the estate agent came around today and valued it at £450,000." What more can be said than well done, Velma – and, can you teach me how to do it? ■

FACT FILE

Names: Kevin and Velma Skingsley
Professions: Charity executive and centre manager
Area: Derbyshire
House type: Three-storey, six-bedroomed detached
House size: 267m²
Build route: Self-managed
Finance: BuildStore Accelerator mortgage
Construction: Natural stone and blockwork
Warranty: NHBC Solo
Build time: 12 months
Land cost: £50,000
Build cost: £115,544
Total cost: £165,544
Current value: £450,000
Cost/m²: £431

63%
COST SAVING

FLOORPLAN

The three-storey house (the attic storey is not shown) contains six bedrooms and a traditional ground floor layout, with three separate living areas.

USEFUL CONTACTS

Self-build manager Chris Turner, Aizlewoods Building Materials: 01623 420121 **Timber merchants** Allen & Orr Ltd: 01246 232859 **Stonemason** Birchover Stone: 01629 650881 **Builders' merchants** Travis Perkins: 01246 271221 **Windows and doors** Frametech: 01246 205577

THE GRASS IS GREENER

Rory and Sylvie Robinson have succeeded in building a family-friendly eco home without blowing their budget.

WORDS: CAROLINE EDNIE
PHOTOGRAPHY: ANDREW LEE

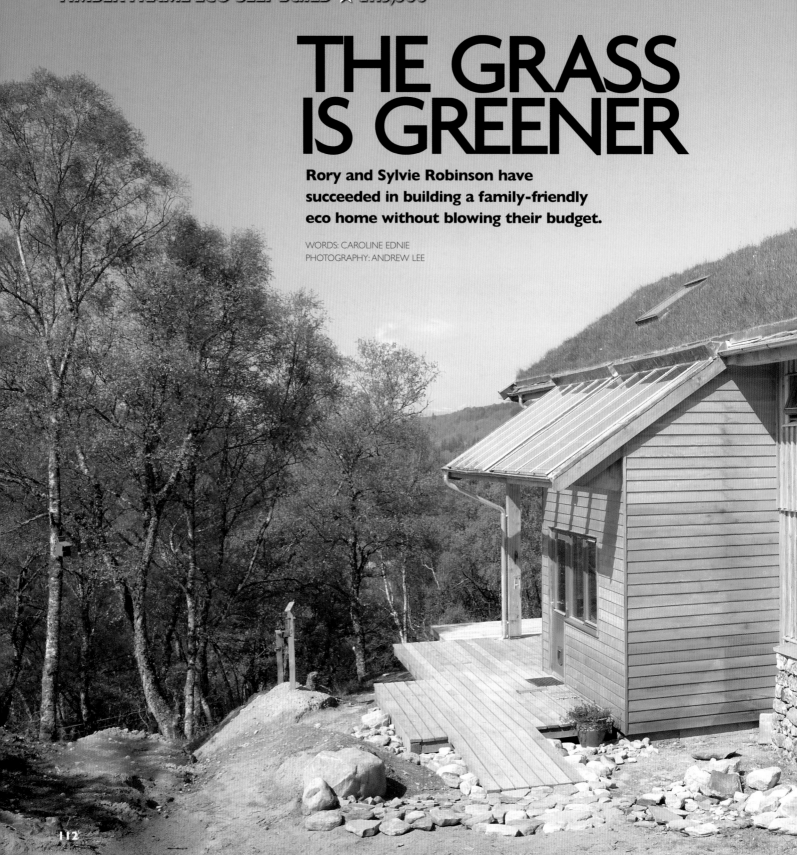

The turf was laid on top of four inches of earth and is designed to act as an insulator, retaining warmth in the house during winter and keeping the interior cool in summer.

AFTER MORE THAN five years searching for a site, a further 18 months living in a caravan, and some heavy-duty hands-on work – including laying a natural turf roof – Rory Robinson proclaims that the new home that he and wife, Sylvie, now share with their three children, Natasha, Manon and Eric, is the ultimate family home. "I think your house should really reflect your philosophy of life, and this one certainly does," he says.

The result of all this patience – and toil – is Alltbeithe, a family eco home (although Rory prefers to refer to it as a "natural" home) set high upon the sloping site of an Inverness-shire woodland. Rory, who helped set up an organic food company when he first arrived in the area around 17 years ago, and Sylvie, a teacher in a local school, admit that this site had not been easy to come by. Indeed after five years of searching, it took a bit of luck

"WE WANTED TO USE AS MUCH LOCAL NATURAL MATERIAL AND AS MANY LOCAL TRADESMEN AS POSSIBLE."

Heat travels up into the open mezzanine area, keeping it warm. The flue also acts as a radiator.

to finally intervene before the couple managed to secure the site. "In 2003 the farmer that owned the surrounding land was selling off pockets, and almost sold the land to someone else, but they pulled out. When the farmer saw the land-seeking advertisement that we had placed in the local paper, he got in touch," explains Rory.

The beautiful hillside one-acre location, which provides the family with their own natural garden, also boasts stunning views. "It was a big attraction to us, and the children love it," says Rory.

In terms of the house itself, Rory and Sylvie originally explored the idea of constructing a standard timber frame kit house. "We thought this would be a cheaper option," explains Rory. "But the kit manufacturers we found weren't flexible enough for our needs. We had a post and beam construction in mind, and we also wanted to build an ecologically efficient house, so we eventually came to the conclusion that we needed an architect." The couple were particularly impressed with the eco homes of Inverness-based architect Neil Sutherland, so they approached him with a few ideas, and Neil agreed to take on the Robinson commission. ➤

The linoleum floor in the kitchen is both practical and ecologically friendly: it's biodegradable and constructed from entirely natural materials.

"We weren't too prescriptive when we went to Neil," continues Rory. "We had a list of no particular priority. We wanted to use as much local natural material and as many local tradesmen as possible. We also assumed materials would be low-toxicity. Points such as orientation were crucial – we wanted the bedrooms to face the east. We also wanted lots of glass overlooking the views of the loch. In addition, we wanted it to be very open plan and over two levels. First time round, Neil came up with plans that were more or less spot on, and the general layout changed very little from then on."

The house was constructed using an untreated Scots Douglas fir post and beam main frame, with spruce softwood panelling in between. The structure is set on a reclaimed drystone basecourse and the house is clad in vertical larch timber – a device that Rory believes reflects the neighbouring trees. Another respectful nod to the surrounding native woodland landscape is the natural turf roof, which appears almost like a wild meadow in its own right – although the solar panels do give away its function. The house is super insulated using Warmcel, which also fits the environmental bill and allows the building to utilise breathing wall technology. Solar energy contributes to the heating of the house passively

Windows and external doors are made from laminated Scandinavian red pine, whilst the house itself is clad in vertical larch timber.

through the extensive glazing to the south and west. This is then stored in the high thermal mass in the floor slab, and also passively in the sun space to the entrance of the house, which opens to the upper floor. Finally, energy is stored actively in the solar panels on the roof, which connect to the domestic hot water tank, and heat everything apart from the underfloor heating.

The house incorporates one level change on the ground floor, which responds to the sloping site. This also forms an effective contrast to the more cellular bedroom and bathroom spaces, which are situated to the east of the house. Externally, a series of timber decks from the principal living spaces further extend these rooms. Two of the children's bedrooms are located downstairs with the master bedroom and bathroom located above on the mezzanine level. Apart from these rooms, the mezzanine has been left open to create a greater sense of space and take advantage of the views.

"Upstairs on the open mezzanine it's lovely and warm because heat travels up. The glazing at the main entrance canopy also adds to this warmth," says Rory. In addition to the solar gain, the Robinsons have

"I DON'T THINK YOU SHOULD IMPOSE STRICT TIMETABLES AND DEADLINES... THE BEST WAY OF GETTING ON IS JUST GOING WITH THE FLOW."

underfloor heating on the ground level. "If I'd been very eco I'd have used a non-fossil fuel, such as a renewable light wood boiler, but I've used wood before and it really is hard work. So we went for oil, and we've only used one tank over the five winter months. The underfloor heating works really wel – it makes the living area so comfortable, and we do spend a lot of time in this part of the house. Our family time centres round preparing and eating our meals, so the kitchen/dining/living area is the heart of the house.

"We see this as our long-term family home, which is why we spent extra on many good-quality finishes: we want to benefit from them for the next 20 years. We took the long view," says Rory. This strategy means that Alltbeithe boasts laminated Scandinavian red pine used by local manufacturer Treecraft for windows and external doors; French oak and Scandinavian Scot's pine floorboards to the upper floor; Scandinavian dressed redwood finishes for internal cills and architrave; a Scottish oak staircase made by local craftsman Adrian Ellis; and linoleum in the living area.

Rory admits, however, that in order to achieve this quality of structural and material finishes, some cost-cutting did have to take place in order to meet the budget's parameters. The kitchen, for example, is off the shelf from MFI. By literally mucking in during construction, the Robinsons also managed to keep costs down. Last summer, after the main frame had been constructed, Rory and Sylvie took on the task of laying the turf roof themselves with the help of a friend, and also had a turf party, where a group of friends came up to the site one Saturday last summer to help the couple with the lifting, carrying and laying of the turf. "Laying it is just like a jigsaw puzzle. I haven't had to maintain it, but our site isn't that exposed to the elements. It's four inches of earth and, for its thickness, it's not a good insulator, but on the other hand it reduces temperature changes — so on a very hot day it won't overcook the house. Primarily it's aesthetic."

The Robinsons also did their fair share of site supervision. "Although the architect supervised at the really important stages, we found ourselves being clerks of work the rest of the time," says Rory.

Although the family are now installed full-time in Alltbeithe, Rory admits that there are still a few finishing touches here and there that need to be done, but makes no attempt to implement a strict timetable. "I don't think you should impose strict timetables and deadlines in rural areas anyway. It's a small community and I think the best way of getting on is just going with the flow." ∎

FACT FILE

Names: Rory and Sylvie Robinson
Professions: Owner of organic food company and teacher
Area: Balnain, Highlands
House type: Detached, four bedroom family house
House size: 135m²
Build route: Self-managed plus architect
Finance: Private
Construction: Douglas fir post and beam frame, with untreated spruce softwood panelling in between
Build time: 18 months

Land cost: £35,000
Build cost: £115,000
Total cost: £150,000
Current value: Unknown
Cost/m²: £851

FIRST FLOOR

GROUND FLOOR

FLOORPLAN

An open plan kitchen dining area – double height – is the focal point of the ground floor, which also houses a bedroom, in addition to the three upstairs.

USEFUL CONTACTS

Architect Neil Sutherland Architects: 01463 709993 **Structural engineer** AF Crudens: 01463 719200 **Main contractor** Kenny Beaton & John Dalgetty: 01463 811327 **Joinery** The Stornoway Trust: 01851 706916 **Cabinet maker, timber supplier, staircase, balustrade and decking** Adrian Ellis: 01456 476268 **Stonemason** Tom Nelson: 01456 450506

BUDGET NEW OAK-FRAMED HOME ★ £55,000

Border Oak's Halfpenny Cottage has a brick chimney and gable ends, which proved ideal for Bill who is a bricklayer by trade.

OAK FRAME VALUE

Bill and Lynn Bradford have built a beautiful three-bedroomed oak-framed cottage almost entirely by themselves.

WORDS: DEBBIE JEFFERY PHOTOGRAPHY: COLIN BARRATT

A BURGLARY FORCED us to leave our family home, where I had lived for most of my life," says Lynn Bradford, who had purchased the house from her parents. "We were asleep at the time and, although we weren't hurt, the place never felt like home after that night. Bill and I had lived in the house for 20 years and had built a number of extensions. We had often discussed self-building, and this seemed like the perfect time to move on."

The couple began hunting for land in the area, and discovered an idyllic plot in a Herefordshire village where they had first met at a dance 30 years before. "Our daughter also lives in the area, and we knew the village very well," Lynn continues. "It is a small, close community of around 70 people, and somewhere we had always wanted to live."

Bill's old school friend is a local farmer who had sold off two plots of land to self-builders, and happened to have one last piece of land available. The Bradfords decided to purchase the quarter of an acre for £55,000 subject to gaining full planning permission and, although it was effectively a greenfield site with fabulous views across the surrounding countryside, planning was approved because it is situated within the designated development plan for the village.

The Bradfords sold their house and most of their belongings before moving into a caravan on the site. "It did feel strange leaving our old house," says Lynn, "but we were both excited about building, and soon got used to living in the caravan. The rain was extremely noisy on the roof and kept us awake, but not having to do any housework was a real bonus!"

Bill is a self-employed bricklayer by trade, who has subcontracted to Border Oak Design and Construction for 16 years. The family-run ➤

119

"WE TALKED THROUGH THE COSTINGS WITH BORDER OAK, AND THEY ESTIMATED £44,000 FOR THE BASIC BUILD – WHICH TURNED OUT TO BE EXTREMELY ACCURATE."

company pioneered the revival of green oak framing, employs almost 200 people and undertakes projects all over the world.

Rural Herefordshire is the heartland of oak frame buildings, and there were already three Border Oak houses in the village. Bill and Lynn knew that they wanted to build a Border Oak house and based their design on the Halfpenny Cottage – a range which features a brick chimney and gable ends.

The Bradfords' house has a spacious lounge and kitchen/breakfast room, cloakroom and utility on the ground floor, with a weatherboarded garage. Upstairs, there is a master bedroom suite, and two further bedrooms which share a bathroom. "We sat down with the designer at Border Oak and changed the layout slightly, so that we have a dressing room and a large en-suite bathroom for the master bedroom above the garage," says Bill. "We talked through the costings with Border Oak, and they estimated £44,000 for the basic build – which turned out to be extremely accurate."

Bill and Lynn hired a track machine and a dumper and spent three weekends preparing the footings and oversite – starting work on February 14. "It wasn't the most romantic Valentine's Day," laughs Lynn. "Bill's idea of a thoughtful gesture was to buy me a van so that I could lug materials home from the builder's merchants!"

The frame was made by Border Oak and then erected in a weekend by Bill and his son, together with friends from the company's frame erection crews. "I had helped them out with baseworks and bricklaying in the past, and they returned the favour," Bill explains. "Our neighbours had gone away for the weekend and couldn't believe their eyes when they got back to see our frame was already up.

"Building the house ourselves was hard work, because we were fitting it in at the weekends, after working a full week at our jobs, and we only had one half day off throughout the entire build," continues Bill, who took a week's holiday to complete the roof, which proved complex due to the inclusion of dormer windows. "Initially, I thought it would take us a couple of years to build the house. As it turned out we were in within ten months, which was a pleasant surprise!"

Known for being a fast worker, Bill completed the external bricklaying using bricks reclaimed from a demolished terrace of houses in Manchester. He chose flush pointing and a lime mortar to help give the cottage an aged

Oak kitchen units were ex-display from a Border Oak show-house, and fit perfectly thanks to a brick wine rack constructed to one corner of the room. ➤

The staircase, windows and internal doors are all idigbo hardwood, stained to give the appearance of oak.

appearance, and particularly enjoyed this aspect of the build. The 100mm thick dense polystyrene infill panels and weatherproofing came with the Border Oak kit, and Bill would fit four or five each evening after work using expanding foam. These are finished with self-coloured render outside and skim plaster inside.

Lynn, who works as a supervisor for a medical firm, took care of most of the paperwork, secured planning, purchased materials and kept meticulous financial records. "Bill is far more practical than I am, but I am a good organiser so we worked well as a team," she explains. "Our son is a plumber by trade, and fitted the bathrooms and laid the underfloor heating on the ground floor. We also had help with the plastering and electrics, but Bill completed the rest of the work himself."

Internally, the house is simple and traditional, with exposed panels of reclaimed bricks in the hallway, and a large fireplace in the lounge which Bill built to Lynn's design. The same bricks, purchased from a local reclamation yard, have been used to form a surround for the range cooker in the kitchen, which is fitted with solid oak kitchen units. These had previously been used in a Border Oak showhouse, and were made to fit by building a brick wine rack to one corner of the room.

"We saved money on the external joinery, which is all idigbo hardwood," says Bill. "Our doors and windows were made by a local joinery firm, who also designed the staircase. I managed to buy some dark stained idigbo internal doors for £600, which I stripped using oxilic acid and paint stripper

"INITIALLY, I THOUGHT IT WOULD TAKE US A COUPLE OF YEARS TO BUILD THE HOUSE. AS IT TURNED OUT, WE WERE IN WITHIN TEN MONTHS, WHICH WAS A PLEASANT SURPRISE!"

and polished by hand. The end result looks similar to oak, and has saved us over £2,000."

The cottage has flagstones in the hallway and kitchen, and kiln-dried oak flooring in the lounge, which works surprisingly well over the underfloor heating. Shortly after the couple moved into the cottage, a fish tank in the lounge cracked, spilling thirty gallons of water over their newly laid oak floor. "We panicked and, sure enough, the oak began to lift when we turned on the underfloor heating," says Bill. "Our insurance didn't cover us, but after a couple of months the floor had all gone back down and was perfect. We were really lucky."

After a hectic build the Bradfords are finally able to relax and appreciate the fruits of their labours. Their new home backs onto open fields where sheep and lambs graze, and Bill loves watching the birds and wildlife. "We really enjoyed the whole build, and it was particularly satisfying doing so much of it ourselves," he says. "We would certainly consider self-building again, once we've had a rest. It has been a real life-changing experience." ■

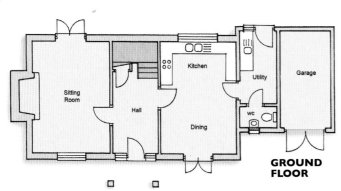

GROUND FLOOR

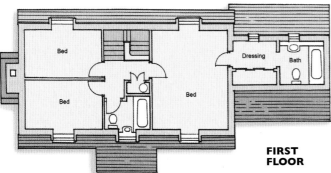

FIRST FLOOR

FLOORPLAN

The cottage is based on Border Oak's Halfpenny range, and has a spacious lounge, a cloakroom, utility and kitchen/breakfast room on the ground floor. Upstairs, there is a master bedroom suite with en-suite and dressing room, with two further bedrooms sharing a bathroom.

GET AN OAK EFFECT

BILL MANAGED TO BUY SOME DARK STAINED IDIGBO INTERNAL DOORS FOR £600, WHICH I STRIPPED USING OXILIC ACID AND PAINT STRIPPER AND POLISHED BY HAND. THE END RESULT LOOKS SIMILAR TO OAK, AND HAS SAVED US OVER £2,000."

FACT FILE

Names: Bill and Lynn Bradford
Professions: Bricklayer and supervisor for medical firm
Area: Herefordshire
House type: Three-bedroomed cottage
House size: 186m^2
Build route: DIY
Construction: Oak frame, reclaimed bricks, slate roof
Warranty: Architect's Certificate
Finance: Private and Halifax self-build mortgage
Build time: Feb '02-Dec '02
Land cost: £55,000
Build cost: £55,000
Total cost: £110,000
House value: £375,000
Cost/m^2: £296

71%
COST SAVING

Cost Breakdown:

Fees	£940
Drainage	£840
Footings and slab	£2,000
Oak frame	£18,000
Reclaimed bricks	£5,000
Roof slates	£5,500
Doors, windows, staircase	£5,933
Kitchen	£500
Electrics	£3,000
Plumbing, heating, sanitaryware	£5,000
Floorboards	£1,000
Flagstones	£2,000
Internal doors	£600
Oak skirtings	£1,800
Roof trusses	£1,200
Glazing units	£1,200
Miscellaneous	£800
TOTAL	**£55,313**

USEFUL CONTACTS

Oak frame and panels Border Oak Design & Construction Ltd: 01568 708752; **Electrics** DTS Ltd: 01544 232799; **Windows, doors, staircase** Chris Bullock Joinery: 01432 264992; **Reclaimed bricks** Border Counties Reclamation: 01584 711484; **Concrete, gravel, stone** Tarmac Western: 01544 230711; **Sanitaryware** City Plumbing: 01432 355885; **Flagstones** Classical Flagstones: 0117 9371960; **Sink and materials** Kingston Building Supplies: 01544 230081; **Woodburner** Countrywide plc: 01432 352244

CURVE APPEAL

Phil and Fiona Groves have created a stunning contemporary home for a remarkably low build cost of just £190,000

WORDS: JASON ORME PHOTOGRAPHY: JEREMY PHILLIPS

HIDDEN AWAY BEHIND an attractive, although hardly earth-shattering, new exterior in a very quiet corner on the Nottinghamshire/Lincolnshire border lies a quite astonishing set of interior spaces that feel like the finest of magazine-spread living brought to life. These stylish, open spaces, with supremely high-quality finishing and the finest of design forethought, would be pretty impressive in the most chic of London dwellings; the fact that this is the East Midlands, they are hidden behind an unassuming traditional-style exterior and that the whole house was built for just £190,000 makes the achievement practically eye-watering.

It is difficult to know where to begin listing the wonders of Phil and Fiona Groves' new home. Building any sort of house these ▶

Phil and Fiona spent time researching their kitchen, eventually finding a company (Odyssey Kitchens 0115 976 1876) that provided cutting-edge kitchen units that were a quarter of the price of some high-end competitors, but which came fully assembled.

The exterior of the house is reasonably traditional to fit in with the local design scheme, although the rear does feature an interesting cedar-clad section above folding sliding doors that open onto a patio area.

days for the bargain price of £633/m² would be a near miracle in its own right, but this tiny figure has created a home that could quite easily have cost five times that.

"We had always done up our previous houses and felt that we wanted to do something a little more ambitious," says Phil. "We initially considered converting a barn and, having put in an offer that morning on a barn that got turned down over the phone, we asked the agent if he had anything else that might be of interest. He said that he had just taken on a plot of land that morning and we went to look straight away."

The site, a greenfield infill plot in a tiny hamlet between Grantham and Newark, looked its worst on the wet November day that the couple visited, but both could see its potential. "I said to Phil that this was going to be quite a project," says Fiona. "We both loved modern open spaces; my parents live in a modern house and I'd always been interested in design, while Phil has a particular passion for American homes."

Although the site came with Outline Planning Permission, Phil and ▶

"WE BOTH LOVED MODERN OPEN SPACES; MY PARENTS LIVE IN A MODERN HOUSE AND I'D ALWAYS BEEN INTERESTED IN DESIGN."

"ONE OF THE JOYS OF THE OPEN PLAN LAYOUT IS THAT, ALTHOUGH THE ROOM ISN'T ACTUALLY USED ALL THAT MUCH, WE STILL GET TO SEE IT ALL THE TIME AND FULLY ENJOY IT."

The main focus of the formal living room is the impressive fireplace (from Diligence www. diligenceinternational. com) with an exposed full-height flue.

we sensed something as controversial as a white-rendered modern home might take ages to get through. We decided to reflect the local red brick and pantile in our exterior design."

Stepping into the new house, the transformation from old to new really takes the breath away. "Visitors are always surprised when they step in," says Fiona. There are, however, odd clues for the astute interior detective in the exterior detailing, not least the two large vertical windows (the bottom of which is folding/sliding, mirroring the window at the other side of the front door), which throw light into the spectacular double-height formal living room. "It really is the centre of the house," says Phil. "We planned the layout around it so that you could see the space from as many places as possible. One of the joys of the open plan layout is that, although the room isn't actually used all that much, we still get to see it all the time and fully enjoy it." The space is focused around an impressive fireplace with exposed full-height flue. The large amount of glazing on the south-facing elevation allows the underfloor-heated space to feel incredibly comfortable even on a cold December day.

While Phil and Fiona got an architect to upgrade their detailed sketches to Building Regulations standard, they decided to employ a builder to bring the house up to shell stage, at which point Phil, having sold his electrical contracting business, decided to work full-time on the house. "He's one of those practical people who is happy to get advice and then tackle the job himself," says Fiona. It was this hands-on approach that was the key to achieving such high-quality interiors without paying high-quality prices. "I think it was the staircase that summed it up most of all," says Phil. "We wanted an elliptical design but getting someone in to design, manufacture and install it would have cost £1,000s. I managed to design it myself, manufacture it and set it in position for a total cost of just £500. It looks great and you would never guess the money we saved."

The same approach went into specifying interior fittings, all of which were researched to within an inch of their lives. "We found a kitchen ➤

Fiona decided to modify the initial scheme, placing the house back in line with the other buildings on the road and enlarging the footprint slightly. "We did consider something much more contemporary on the outside," explains Phil, "but we knew

The large amount of glazing on the south-facing elevation allows the underfloor-heated space to feel incredibly comfortable even on a cold day.

that this was a village dominated by traditional-style houses and, while the planners didn't necessarily indicate that they wanted something in keeping,

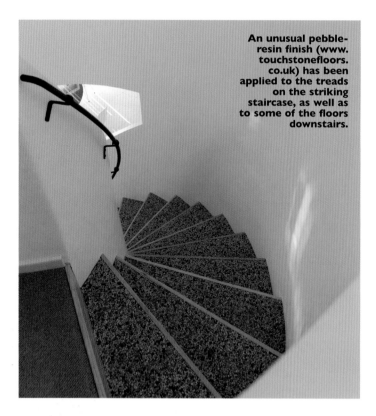

An unusual pebble-resin finish (www.touchstonefloors.co.uk) has been applied to the treads on the striking staircase, as well as to some of the floors downstairs.

"GETTING SOMEONE IN TO DESIGN, MANUFACTURE AND INSTALL THE STAIRCASE WOULD HAVE COST £1,000S. I MANAGED TO DESIGN IT, MANUFACTURE IT AND SET IT IN POSITION FOR A TOTAL COST OF JUST £500."

company that provided cutting-edge units that were not only a quarter of the price of high-end competitors but came fully made up," explains Phil. "The limestone tiles that we've had throughout the ground floor were imported directly from Alicante at a fraction of the price of other ones we saw."

Phil took over the project, employing a local brickie and, with the help of a friend and Fiona's father as labourers, they were able to undertake most of the work between them, the first job being to install all the windows. At this stage the couple enjoyed a stroke of luck and managed to rent the house next door for the final six months of the project. "It was a lot of fun and very handy being so close to the site, in terms of being able to work long hours and from a security point of view," Phil says. "I had a good go at doing things well and learnt a lot along the way. Making the curved stud walls was very difficult – I had to score the plasterboard and wet it to make it more malleable – but I got there in the end. Then, of course, as soon as I'd finished I found out that you can buy flexible plasterboard! We got contractors in where we needed them and managed to do as good a job as a building contractor, but with a bit more imagination."

For a first self-build project the interior finishes in particular show an ambition and confidence in material specification that usually only serial self-builders enjoy. An unusual pebble-resin finish has been applied to some of the downstairs floors and the treads on the staircase – and are a real triumph. Likewise, Phil bought four sheets of ash-laminated mdf, put them on a track and for £200 has a set of stylish sliding doors for the built-in wardrobe.

"We've really enjoyed the project and love living in the spaces that we've created. We're proud of the level of finish we've achieved and while there are always things that we'd do differently, we've learnt a lot – so much so that we're now about to start the next one," says Phil. Meanwhile, a rather wobbly homemade cardboard model of a new curved staircase sits proudly on the coffee table, ready to be called into action. ■

"WE'RE PROUD OF THE LEVEL OF FINISH WE'VE ACHIEVED – SO MUCH SO THAT WE'RE NOW ABOUT TO START THE NEXT ONE."

FACT FILE

Names: Phil and Fiona Groves
Professions: Electrician and consultant in country access and recreation
Area: Lincolnshire
House type: Four-bedroomed home
House size: 300m²
Build route: Main builder and DIY
Construction: Masonry and brick
Build time: April '03-Aug '04
Land cost: £100,000
Build cost: £190,000
Total cost: £290,000
House value: £600,000
Cost/m²: £633

52%
COST SAVING

FLOORPLAN

GROUND FLOOR

The whole house is laid out around the double-height living area, which is open plan onto the entrance hallway and kitchen. Upstairs, the curved staircase gives access to four bedrooms and has a landing overlooking the living space.

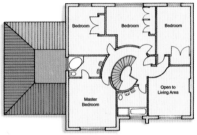

FIRST FLOOR

CREATING CURVES

Curved walls add a real sense of softness to a house but are notoriously difficult to create well. Most plasterboards can be curved when wetted but it is very much an inexact science – the best option is to specify one of the new generation of curved plasterboards (such as the 6mm-thick Contour wallboard from Lafarge www.lafargeplasterboard.co.uk). Lafarge also produces a range of supports such as Flex Track to keep the boards in place. Other suppliers include Gyproc.

USEFUL CONTACTS

Kitchen Odyssey Kitchens Nottingham: 0115 9761876 **Furniture** Atomic Interiors: 0115 941 5577 www.atomicinteriors.co.uk **Underfloor heating** Eco Hometec: 01302 722266 www.eco-hometec.co.uk **Limestone flooring** Alicante Stone: www.alicantestone.com **Stone** resin floors Touchstone Flooring: 01709 382513 www.touchstonefloors.co.uk **Woodburner** Diligence: 01364 654716 www.diligenceinternational.com **Windows** I-D-Systems: 01603 408804 www.i-d-systems.co.uk **Bathrooms** www.victoria-plumb.com www.bathstore.com

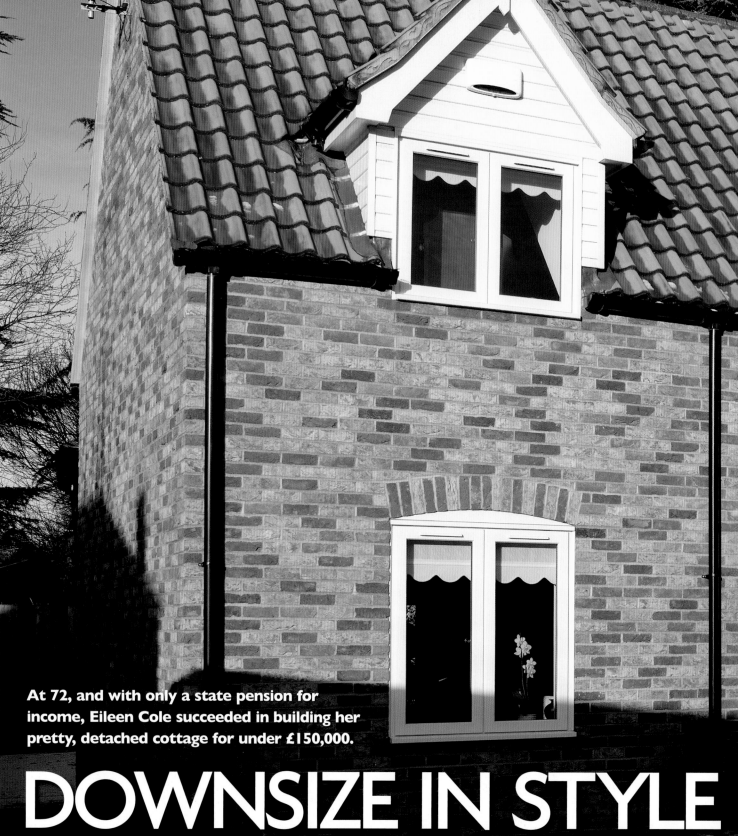

At 72, and with only a state pension for income, Eileen Cole succeeded in building her pretty, detached cottage for under £150,000.

DOWNSIZE IN STYLE

WORDS: DEBBIE JEFFERY PHOTOGRAPHY: JEREMY PHILLIPS

The tiled porch and weatherboarded dormers serving the two upstairs bedrooms give the house a pretty, cottage-style look.

NOTHING CAN BE more wonderful than seeing skilled people giving their best work to produce a building to be proud of," enthuses Eileen Cole of her recent self-build project. At 72, and with only a state pension for income, Eileen decided to build a new cottage in her garden and was impressed by just how conscientious all of the tradesmen proved to be. She took on the role of project manager and thoroughly enjoyed the whole process.

"I've built my own home twice before, so it wasn't a totally alien experience," she explains. "The first project was quite a large house which I built with my husband. He joined my two brothers to set up a building firm, but sadly died after we'd only been living there for two years. I needed to downsize and find somewhere more affordable, so I bought a piece of land in a village and went on to build again. In some ways it was a kind of therapy."

As a director of the family building firm, Eileen was also involved in constructing a two-bedroomed cottage in Spalding for her friend – the renowned strongman and athlete Geoff Capes. "When Geoff decided to sell his house and buy something bigger, we determined to exchange homes, because by that time I wanted to live in the centre of town," explains Eileen. "I lived in his old home for several years before I got itchy feet again."

Eileen found that her large garden was becoming increasingly difficult to maintain, but wanted to remain close to amenities, and came up with the idea of applying for planning permission to build a new home suited to her needs. The garden site is located in a Conservation Area, so certain restrictions applied, and Eileen's architect, John Cooper, devised a simple L-shaped plan with a single storey kitchen, which would create a sunny rear courtyard and maximise the plot.

"Geoff had bought an extra piece of garden from some neighbours, and I had to build on the lawn behind their existing concrete block garage, ▶

"I NEEDED TO DOWNSIZE SO I BOUGHT A PIECE OF LAND IN A VILLAGE AND WENT ON TO BUILD AGAIN. IN SOME WAYS IT WAS A KIND OF THERAPY."

The main open plan living space houses the kitchen, a living area and a dining room, and has two sets of patio doors leading out to a courtyard garden. There is an additional living room the other side of the hall.

135

Internal doors, skirtings and architrave have been matched to the stylish oak staircase.

but it turned out to be a blessing in disguise as it actually affords me some privacy," says Eileen. "I got permission to paint the garage wall and grow climbing plants up it, so now it really doesn't look at all bad. The house itself is totally different from any of my previous projects, and the red pantiles, weatherboarded dormers and entrance porch create quite a pretty cottage effect."

A surveyor oversaw the two-year building project, but it was Eileen who employed the various subcontractors, purchased materials and organised the accounts — continuing to live in her old home.

Eileen's family and friends were a great support and her niece's husband, Dick Whitmore, took on the role of bricklayer and recommended several tradesmen.

"At first I thought that I could build the house for about £120,000," she recalls, "but then I fell in love with some bespoke hardwood windows and doors, which did push up the overall cost. The other big expense was all of the oak joinery inside the house. I felt that off-the-peg internal doors looked a bit flimsy, and asked my joiner friend for a quote to build some in oak. I soon realised that if you choose oak doors you also need oak door linings, skirtings, architrave and staircase."

Determined not to scrimp, Eileen also chose underfloor heating for the ground floor, which has been laid under ceramic floor tiles throughout. The main focus of the new house is the comfortable living kitchen, which opens onto the rear courtyard through patio doors. A utility room

"THE LAYOUT WAS PLANNED SO THAT I COULD LIVE ON THE GROUND FLOOR IN FUTURE, SHOULD I NEED TO."

accommodates Eileen's kitchen appliances, freeing up plenty of space in the relatively compact kitchen.

"It is quite a small house, but it suits me perfectly," she says. "I'm lucky enough to have five children and ten grandchildren, so having a second bedroom and en-suite on the first floor is really useful when people come to stay.

"The layout was planned so that I could live on the ground floor in future, should I need to. The study could become a bedroom and the wetroom is very easy to use."

Despite using high-quality materials and fittings, Eileen managed to keep the final build costs to under £150,000, purchasing almost everything from a single builders' merchant, and benefiting from discounts.

"There were times when nothing got done for several weeks, but I wanted the best craftsmen and realised that I would have to wait," Eileen says. "My patience was rewarded because the finish is such high quality. I pinch myself every morning, not quite believing that I'm living here; but my children worry that I'll get bored and want to do it again. They're used to moving me from place to place, and know just how much I love to build!" ■

FACT FILE

Name: Eileen Cole
Profession: Retired
Area: Lincolnshire
House type: Two-bedroomed detached cottage-style house
House size: 123m²
Build route: Self-managed with subcontractors
Finance: Private
Construction: Brick and block, pantiles
Build time: Jan '04-Feb '06
Land value: £70,000
Build cost: £142,000
Total cost: £212,000
Current value: £350,000
Cost/m²: £1,154

39%
COST SAVING

Cost Breakdown:

Materials	£41,450
Raft foundation	£9,200
Roofing	£5,000
Electrical	£5,000
Sanitaryware	£3,200
External doors and windows	£12,600
Plumbing and heating	£9,000
Floor tiles	£2,200
Kitchen	£2,350
Labour	£52,000
TOTAL	**£142,000**

"I PINCH MYSELF EVERY MORNING, NOT QUITE BELIEVING THAT I'M LIVING HERE!"

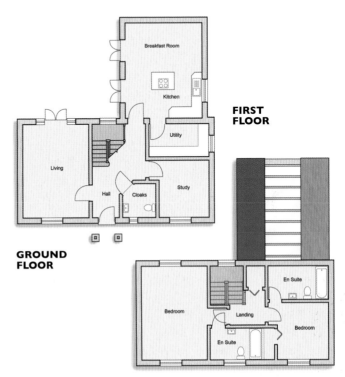

FIRST FLOOR

GROUND FLOOR

FLOORPLAN

Designed so that Eileen could live solely on the ground floor if required, the main focus of the house is the living kitchen with a neighbouring utility. There is a separate study, sitting room and wetroom on this level, and both first floor bedrooms have their own en-suite bathrooms.

USEFUL CONTACTS

Architect John Cooper: 01406 423762 **Builder** Dick Whitmore: 01775 710171 **Construction** Ulric Hilliam: 01406 540720 **Structural engineer** Steven Kidd: 01775 769563 **Doors and windows** George Barnsdale & Sons: 01775 823000 **Financial services** Lynas Vokes: 01406 422788 **Builders' merchant** Jackson Building Centres: 01775 766004 **Joiner and carpenter** Jonathan Amess: 01775 760793 **Roofing contractor** Manor Roofing Ltd: 01778 346666 **Decorators** Geoff Paynter and Keith Rhodes: 01406 424705 **Plumbing and heating** Julian Smith: 01778 421952 **Fencing** Aztec Fencing: 01775 724567 **Oak internal doors and staircase** JT Ward Joinery Ltd: 01406 423517 **Coving** John Belsham: 01406 425444 **Plastering** Paul Tibbs: 01945

440293 **Floor tiles** Contraband Tile & Wallpaper Centre: 01778 347809 **Tiles** Sackstore (Boston Tile Ltd): 01205 310102 **Surveyor** Neil Clarke & Associates: 01775 711344 **Flooring contractors** Abledell Ltd: 01733 577877 **Plant hire** South Lincs Scaffolding: 01205 363366 **Crane hire** Crowland Cranes Ltd: 01733 211722 **Sand, stone and gravel** Bullimore Sand & Gravel Ltd: 01778 423309 **WCs and basins** Ideal Standard: 01482 346461 **Redland Norfolk pantiles** Lafarge Roofing Ltd: 01306 872000 **Toronto Buttermilk kitchen** The Symphony Group plc: 0870 120 8000 **Baths** Harold Moore & Son Ltd: 0114 233 6161 **Tarmac** TopPave paving Brett Landscaping & Building Products: 01634 222188 **Sofa and pouffe** Furniture Village: 0800 783 0830

Serial self-builders Joan and Barry van Nierop have built a timber-framed home on an awkward sloping site – all for just £740/m².

FIFTH TIME LUCKY

WORDS: DEBBIE JEFFERY   PHOTOGRAPHY: JEREMY PHILLIPS

IT TOOK ME a few years to persuade Joan that we should build another new house," says Barry van Nierop. "She loved the location of our old home with its views across the Cheshire Plain towards the Welsh mountains, but the dishwasher and cooker needed replacing, and it's always been my philosophy that when appliances wear out, it's time to move on."

Over the years, Barry and Joan have built four traditional brick and block houses for themselves and their three children, but this time Barry, a retired developer, was keen to use timber frame and to design a house with the couple's three young grandchildren in mind.

The van Nierops purchased a run-down 1940s asbestos prefab in Kelsall, the Cheshire village where they have lived since 1978, with the intention of demolishing the existing property and building a brand new house. The long, half-acre plot sloped significantly, dictating the width and design of the new house, and the solution was to build over three storeys – maximising the available space by creating two additional bedrooms and a bathroom in the roof served by dormer windows.

Barry and his business partner Dennis had previously built a number of small developments of Potton timber-framed houses and he was very impressed with the speed of erection, high levels of insulation and quality finishes. He decided to loosely base the design for his own house on the Waterford from Potton's Shire range, using an architect to add a second storey, completely reorganise the layout and create a totally bespoke design.

The existing bungalow was less than half the size of the proposed 325m² ➤

Bespoke kitchen units were made by Italian company SDB Kitchens of Chester. A family room is stepped down from the kitchen/breakfast room and acts as an informal TV lounge.

house, and it took six months before the planners and parish council finally approved the van Nierops' plans. A specialist company was then contracted to demolish and safely remove the asbestos prefab, leaving Barry to prepare the footings, retaining walls and drainage, with extra-deep foundations constructed beneath what is now the patio to compensate for the slope of the site.

"Foundations and levels need to be extremely precise for a timber frame," he explains, "and I was further helped by our daughter, Tineke, who had just completed her A levels and decided to take a year out before university. She tackled everything from mixing concrete and wheeling barrows to building blockwork, and it made the whole thing

far more enjoyable being able to work together on site. We bought a temporary house just across the road which we used during the build, and living so close by meant that I could get a very early start and carry on quite late into the night."

The ground floor is block and beam construction with 80mm of Styrofoam on a plastic damp-proof membrane covering the beams and topped off with an 18mm chipboard floating floor. This increases the insulative qualities of the property and was one of the reasons Barry converted to building using a timber frame. "A fast build speed was another important factor, because we were going to go away for Christmas and needed the house to be secure and weathertight before we left," he continues.

"Potton began erecting the frame at the end of November, so it was a huge undertaking to make sure that the building was roofed, glazed and locked up in just four weeks. I think it was a personal record for the

 ━━━ ★

HUNG TILING

Slates or tiles can create decorative finishes to new and refurbished properties when hung vertically on the walls, gables or on dormer windows. Once designed as a

means of protection against the elements, this traditional form of cladding is now used to add character and individuality to a property, in addition to providing

a useful rain screen. There is a huge range of styles and colours, and vertical tiling is suitable for both timber frame and masonry construction using tiling battens.

"THE DRAWBACK OF BUILDING A THREE-STOREY HOUSE WAS THAT FIRE REGULATIONS STIPULATED WE FIT DOORS VIRTUALLY EVERYWHERE."

builders, and when we came back in January the dry-liners stayed with us and worked simultaneously with the bricklayers – which meant that the whole build was completed very quickly."

Clay tiles were chosen for the roof, with Barry and Joan specifying Eternit's double-cambered Acme plain tiles in addition to valley tiles, vent adaptors, cockscomb crested ridge tiles and fleur-de-lys finials. Bullnose ornamental tiles have been hung vertically on the dormer windows and gables, with ornamental tiles creating banding and diamond patterns, which have also been reproduced on the smaller gable dormers.

"We knew that the local planning authority would be taking a keen interest in the property, particularly in view of its prominent position," Barry says. "Attention to detail was vital and we were keen to use high-quality natural products wherever possible."

With Barry taking charge of the construction work, Joan was able to concentrate on the interior and garden design, choosing colour schemes and fixtures and fittings throughout the house and making the curtains and soft furnishings herself.

The sloping nature of the site dictated some of the room layouts. "The kitchen/breakfast room has been positioned to the rear of the house, with two steps down into the family room to follow the contours of the site and create a split-level space," Joan explains. "We tend to spend the majority of our time there, and it's ideal when the family visit because you can cook and still remain in contact with everyone."

"We enjoy open plan living and hate doors, but the drawback of building a three-storey house was that fire regulations stipulated we should fit doors virtually everywhere," says Barry, who would have preferred the dining room to remain open plan to the entrance hall. Despite this fact, the couple have drawn on their extensive self-build experience to create a home which has a number of distinctive trademark features.

"Building your own home allows you to specify these sort of details, and it's such a rewarding experience that I'm sure this won't be our last timber frame self-build. We will probably down-size and build a house for our retirement next time. When the dishwasher needs replacing, Barry will suggest a new project and we'll be moving on again!" ■

GROUND FLOOR

FIRST FLOOR

SECOND FLOOR

FACT FILE

Names: Barry and Joan van Nierop
Professions: Retired
Area: Cheshire
House type: Six-bedroomed detached house
House size: 325m²
Build route: Timber frame kit, DIY and self-managed subcontractors
Construction: Timber frame, brick and tile cladding, clay roof tiles
Finance: Private
Build time: Sept '02-June '03
Land cost: £184,000
Build cost: £241,000
Total cost: £425,000
House value: £750,000
Cost/m²: £742

43% COST SAVING

Cost Breakdown:

Fees	£8,000
Engineering	£11,000
Timber frame kit	£55,000
Roofing	£15,000
Bricks, masonry, labour	£28,000
Scaffold	£3,500
Dry-lining	£12,000
Sanitaryware	£8,500
Plumbing and heating	£13,000
Windows	£11,000
Electrics	£9,000
Security	£4,000
Externals, groundworks and labour	£17,000
Kitchen and appliances	£16,500
Fitted bedroom and bathroom furniture	£12,000
Render	£2,500
Painting and decorating	£5,000
Tiling	£10,000
TOTAL	**£241,000**

FLOORPLAN

The ground floor is divided into an informal split-level kitchen/breakfast/family room to the rear and a formal lounge and dining room to either side of the entrance hall. The first floor master bedroom has a dressing room and en-suite, with a sewing room for Joan, a study for Barry and a guest bedroom, while daughter Tineke's bedroom and bathroom is on the second floor, together with a further guest room.

USEFUL CONTACTS

Timber frame kit Potton Limited: 01480 401401 **Architect** Northwest Design Associates: 01829 751555 **Bricks** Terca: 0161 873 7701 **Tiles** Porcelanosa: 0800 915 4000 **Windows** Rehau Ltd: 01989 762600 **Kitchen** SDB Kitchens: 01244 335994 **Heating engineers** Heating Water Services Ltd: 0151 342 8354 **Roof tiles** Eternit Building Materials: 01763 264686 **Sanitaryware** Roca Ltd: 01530 830080 **Taps, shower** Hansgrohe: 0870 770 1972 **Block and beam floor** Merseybeams Ltd: 0151 334 7346 **Sanitaryware and heating** Atlas Heating: 0161 864 3610

Despite the unashamedly contemporary appearance of the house, located in a street of 19th century terraces, planning permission was not a problem.

IT'S HIP TO BE SQUARE

Richard Dudzicki and Eva Edohen have built a striking contemporary urban home using modern eco-friendly building techniques.

WORDS: ANGELA PERTUSINI   PHOTOGRAPHY: TIMOTHY SOAR

MY WIFE WANTED a Victorian place," reveals Richard Dudzicki. Being a loyal husband, his face remains deadpan as he explains this but he can't help lending a restrained sigh to the memory. "She'd grown up with Victorian houses," he adds hastily. "It was what she was comfortable with – but, after a little gentle persuasion, she agreed to this."

This is the home that Richard, an architect, eventually built for himself and lawyer wife Eva, and it has about as much in common with Victoriana as an iPod. An appealing slab of modernity in an otherwise unremarkable street of plain 19th century terraces, the house makes no attempt to ally itself to its neighbours – Richard thoughtfully provided the door number but there is little doubt which house is his. "As it's the first house in the road, it's OK to do something different," he says. "It's a punctuation mark."

Quite how the house came into being is a slightly meandering tale which combines the two great driving forces in London property ownership: spiralling rents and a growing family. Richard would have us

believe the house is almost accidental, but this seems a little disingenuous – I mean who wouldn't have thought of building on such a plot?

Nonetheless, the opportunity that he grabbed in 1999 was to buy a former light industrial, two-storey building on a Dulwich side-street. He applied for and received consent to convert it into a residential unit, only to decide almost immediately to move his practice there from Clerkenwell, then the capital of the UK's dot.com boom and subsequently an area of increasingly greedy landlords.

Almost inevitably, the unit became too cramped as both the Dudzicki practice and the Dudzicki family expanded. In 2003, with the arrival of his daughter, Richard began to cast around for a solution and, more in the spirit of hope than expectation, applied for permission to demolish a pair of garages in front of the unit and build a home. The land had a planning history of stock car racing and, Richard claims, was such a scrappy and unattractive piece of fly-tipped suburban decay, that building on it hadn't occurred to him before. The council was supportive, as were ➤

143

The kitchen features red lacquered units, a Corian worktop and a lino floor over underfloor heating.

most of the local residents. A new house, even a scary, contemporary one, has to be a lot more desirable than the ramshackle garages and festering mattresses that were already there. In property value terms, the perennial refuge of the nimby, it could only improve matters.

"One neighbour was very difficult about party wall consents," says Richard, "but he doesn't even live here – he rents out the property. I think everyone else was just relieved that something was going to be done with this horrible eyesore."

And so, in terms of appearance, once he had dismissed his wife's wishlist of sash windows and London stocks, Richard had a pretty free hand and took advantage of that to create a sleek, three-storey box which soars out of an unpromisingly small footprint.

"ONE NEIGHBOUR WAS VERY DIFFICULT...
EVERYONE ELSE WAS RELIEVED THAT
SOMETHING WAS GOING TO BE DONE
WITH THIS EYESORE."

Ah yes, the footprint. Hemmed in by an electrical sub-station at the rear and the street's building line to the fore, the house isn't as generously proportioned as most self-builders would hope for. Richard's open plan design ideal usually relies on, well, a bit more space to be open in. Once Building Control got on board and demanded the necessary but irksome ground floor WC, a wall separating the entrance from the living area and a door on the kitchen, the available space had dwindled even more. But, by using an extremely simple palette of glass, bold red kitchen units and white everything else, together with a crafty layout, the feeling of space is generous.

Upstairs there are two bedrooms and bathrooms and, on the top floor, a wonderful eyrie of a chill-out zone (ready to be dragooned, together with the adjacent utility room, into service as the master bedroom and en-suite when the couple's second baby arrives shortly). Huge, full-length windows dominate one wall and a large balcony wraps around two sides of the room, giving superb rooftop views.

Having spent almost two years planning the build, the actual construction in 2005 went remarkably smoothly, taking less than nine months from breaking ground to moving in. Environmental concerns led Richard to opt for SIPs (structural insulated panels) which create walls from super-efficient insulation sandwiched between sheets of ply. Although his contractor had never built using SIPs before, he had worked with Richard in the past, who was impressed enough to pay for him and ➤

The clutter-free, sleek wet room not only makes the most of the space available, but the use of glass and built-in sanitaryware increases the feeling of it, too.

his team to attend a two-day course to learn more about the method. A few weeks later, the walls of the house arrived on two pallets and were up in less than a fortnight.

As well as being relatively problem-free, it was also a sensationally cheap build – the land came more-or-less free with the old factory unit he bought for £40,000, and the house cost only £148,570 to build. On such a tight budget, Richard has done a fabulous job of sourcing cheap but chic finishes for the home and the only thing that makes him really groan is the £8,000 he had to pay a utility company with a local monopoly to connect the house to the water mains a couple of metres away. Anyone

would struggle to make a loss with those numbers but Richard also hit the jackpot by buying into East Dulwich in the first place, a suburb of increasingly high prices and aspirations.

By anyone's standards this house is a success. The fact that it fits so much into so little is extremely impressive and it does so while maintaining an admirable appearance of calm and simplicity. But it may not remain a small house for too much longer. Despite a serendipitous beginning, Richard is beginning to display imperialist tendencies towards his neighbourhood: having converted the light industrial unit and built over the garages, he has now bought up a plot next door, a former single-storey gallery building. Plans are still hazy at this stage but another residential project is in the offing, possibly a similar house but faced in brick rather than cool white render and iroko cladding. He could just sell it on, of course, but the Dudzickis are toying with the idea of linking the two properties via a bridge in order to grab a little more living space.

It's a thrillingly daring idea and it would be wonderful if it happened. But Richard Dudzicki's neighbours might begin to feel a bit nervous about where he will cast his net next... ■

Sliding doors lead to a private courtyard area, complete with a mature olive tree.

"IT WAS A SENSATIONALLY CHEAP BUILD – THE LAND CAME MORE-OR-LESS FREE AND THE HOUSE COST ONLY £148,570 TO BUILD."

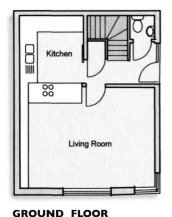
GROUND FLOOR

Kitchen

Living Room

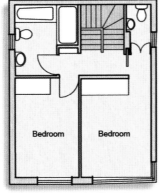
FIRST FLOOR

Bedroom

Bedroom

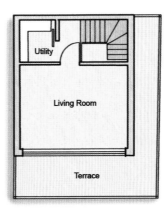
SECOND FLOOR

Utility

Living Room

Terrace

FLOORPLAN

The three-storey home features an open plan kitchen/dining area at ground level with the main living accommodation making the most of the balcony space.

FACT FILE

Names: Richard Dudzicki and Eva Edohen
Professions: Architect and lawyer
Area: Dulwich
House type: Two-bed, three-storey contemporary home
House size: 98m²
Build route: Main contractor
Finance: Private
Construction: SIPs, with STO render
Build time: Feb '05-Oct '05
Land cost: £40,000
Build cost: £148,570
Total cost: £188,570
Current value: £400,000
Cost/m²: £1,516

53%
COST SAVING

Cost Breakdown:

Demolition and site clearance	£3,600
Substructure	£12,800
Superstructure	£74,000
Finishes	£15,400
Fittings and furnishings	£18,200
Services	£8,470
External works	£15,300
TOTAL	**£148,570**

URBAN ARCHITECTURE

Richard and Eva's new home is a remarkable achievement on its merits – brave, radical architecture that perfectly adds to the street scene; use of eco-friendly SIPs that mean super-fast build times and lower energy bills to boot; re-use of a grotty urban site; and a build budget to make any self-builder in the UK jealous. When combined with the clever use of the most modest of footprints to create a home that not only comfortably meets their family's needs but also provides bags of open, light, indulgent living spaces, it is a clear blueprint for affordable, clever, small homes that feel anything but pinched.

USEFUL CONTACTS

Architect RDA UK: 020 8299 2222 **Main contractor** DKBS Ltd: 0207 267 7567 **Builders** JCP Builders: 07957 296928 **Structural engineer** CEC Engineers: 0208 679 5621 **Building control** MLM Building Control: 0207 613 7500 **Roofing** CU.TECH: 01732 822064 **Windows and doors** Velfac: 01223 897100 **SIPs** Kingspan TEK: 01544 387361 **Render** STO-Render: 0208 554 7937 **Landscape designer** James Lee Landscape & Garden Design: 0208 693 9391

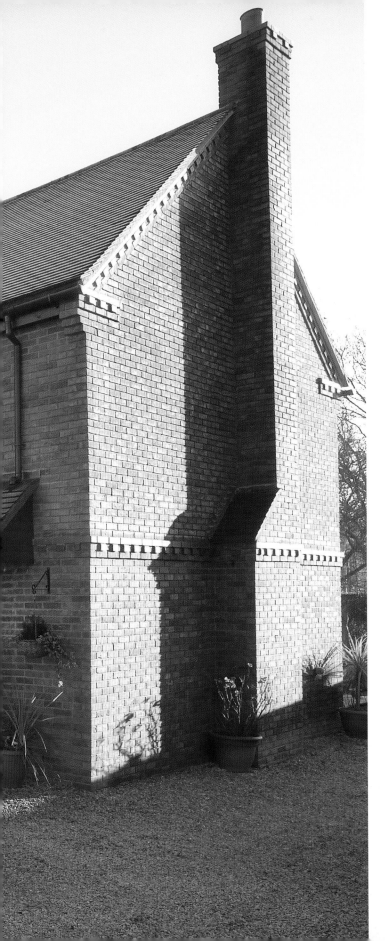

WORDS: DEBBIE JEFFERY   PHOTOGRAPHY: MARK WELSH

With help from their family, Sandra and Eric Dolby have built a four-bedroomed home to a remarkably low budget.

FAMILY AFFAIR

I WAS BROUGHT up on building sites," laughs Sandra Dolby. "My father has always been a keen self-builder, and I have memories of enjoying playing on site with my sisters while he was building. Dad's experience was invaluable when Eric and I decided to build our own house – we simply couldn't have done it without him. He was our architect, project manager and builder all rolled into one. We can never repay him for what he's done."

Sandra and Eric's new four-bedroomed house has been constructed almost entirely by the family, which enabled them to complete the 150m² detached property for an incredible £39,600. Sandra's father, architect Norman Tomson, has been a guiding force behind the project, designing the house and working alongside the Dolbys.

"I have built 12 houses over the past 30 years for myself and my three daughters," Norman says. "I left school and trained at technical college for three years as a bricklayer, also learning carpentry and plumbing, before studying to become an architect. When I built my first house I involved subcontractors, but was so dissatisfied with their work that I thought I could do better myself!"

It was Norman who first suggested that Sandra and Eric should build their own house. "We had a phone call from Dad, who told us that a site was coming onto the market near us, and we had just a few hours to make a decision," says Sandra. "The land was only around the corner from where we lived and already had planning permission for a house, which my father ➤

had designed for a client. When they decided to sell the plot, they offered him first refusal. We knew immediately that we wanted to go ahead."

Eric and Sandra paid £37,000 for the land, which was part of a garden and had been granted detailed planning permission for a brick and block house. They worked with Norman to adapt the design so that the house could be built in timber frame. A study on the ground floor has been omitted, which allows for a spacious utility room next to the kitchen, a downstairs shower room and a cloakroom. There is a separate dining room and a dual-aspect lounge, which runs the full width of the house and leads out into the rear garden through patio doors.

Calculations were prepared by a structural engineer; the plans were passed and work began on site straight away. The Dolbys employed the services of a JCB and driver to dig the foundations, two bricklayers for the external skin of brickwork, a heating engineer to commission the boiler, and a plasterer to finish the ceilings. Other than this they undertook every aspect of the physical work themselves – from pegging out the site and levelling the concrete, to laying the underfloor heating and decorating.

"YOU HAVE TO BE PREPARED TO WORK EVERY EVENING AND AT WEEKENDS AND TO GIVE UP YOUR HOLIDAYS."

The staircase was made by Norman and Eric in yellow pine, and cost just £500 for the timber.

"My interpretation of 'self-build' is for the client to carry out about 85% of the work, using the minimum of subcontract labour," says Norman, who is now in his seventies. "We don't purchase timber frame kits from recognised suppliers, but design and construct all the panels on site. We can make and erect the frames for a detached house in just two weeks. It is far from difficult providing your drawings clearly show all the dimensions, the centres of the studs and panel sizes."

Norman worked with Eric to produce the 140mm x 38mm timber frame panels in CLS (Canadian Lumbar Standard) timber, which was fully treated with timber preservative. To cut and erect the roof timbers took them a further week, with Sandra helping out when she could, following a back injury caused by shovelling concrete.

"You have to be prepared to work every evening and at weekends and to give up your holidays," says Eric, "but building in timber frame is very satisfying as it goes up so quickly, and the whole house was finished in about a year."

Norman spent a great deal of time helping on site, with Sandra and Eric's son, Lee, and daughter, Gemma, also lending a hand. The roof was felted and battened to create a watertight shell, and the bricklayers worked outside while the family tackled the plumbing and carpentry, and Lee undertook the wiring. Underfloor heating pipes were laid in routed chipboard on both the ground and first floors and connected by the family, ➤

Eric built the carcasses for the kitchen units, purchasing inexpensive doors from B&Q.

"IT IS HARD WORK, AND YOU HAVE TO BE PREPARED TO STICK AT IT, BUT WHAT COULD BE MORE REWARDING THAN KNOWING YOU HAVE BUILT YOUR OWN HOME?"

with a plumber employed to make the final connection to the boiler.

"As soon as the bricklayers got up to roof level Eric and myself did all the roof tiling, using plain concrete tiles," says Norman. "Eric worked up on the roof and I organised materials and shouted instructions! We glazed the windows ourselves and hung the doors. Over the years I have built up a nice little workshop, which came in handy."

The family found one of the main problems involved getting materials delivered on time, and Norman would spend hours waiting on the site, which was secured with close-boarded fencing to help prevent theft.

When it came to fixing and jointing the plasterboard lining on the timber frame walls, he was already something an expert. He had attended courses on dry lining, and had also received advice from British Gypsum, who had sent a demonstrator to a previous site on request. "I found this very useful, and was then able to show other people how to use and finish the jointing materials," he says. "We did draw the line

at the ceilings, however, and paid a plasterer to skim these for us."

Eric was responsible for building the carcasses for the kitchen units, which have been fitted with inexpensive B&Q doors for a total of just £500. He also built the fire surround in the sitting room from painted MDF. By undertaking so much of the labour themselves, the couple have managed to complete their house for less than £40,000, with the property now valued at £275,000. With help from Norman they were able to fund the project privately, allowing them to remain in their home throughout the build.

"Selling our previous house proved to be the most stressful part of the entire project," says Sandra. "There were no major problems with the actual build, and we are an extremely close family, so working together was fine — there were no arguments."

Norman feels that more people should be inspired to tackle their own self-builds, and has recently been appointed a member of the Local Authority Affordable Housing Committee for the town of Uppingham in Rutland. He proposes to teach groups of around six people how to construct their own homes using his timber frame method.

"I would love to show others how to overcome the problems encountered on a typical self-build site," he explains. "With a little help, they should gain enough confidence to tackle the whole thing themselves. It is hard work, and you have to be prepared to stick at it, but what could be more rewarding than knowing you have built your own home?" ■

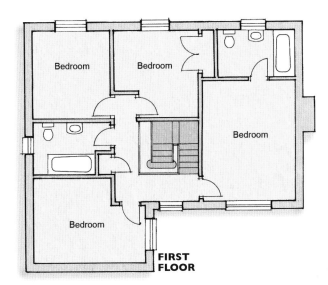

Bedroom

Bedroom

Bedroom

Bedroom

FIRST FLOOR

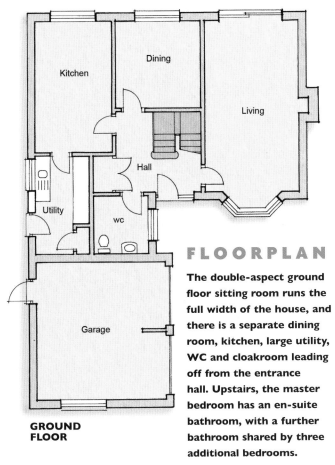

Kitchen

Dining

Living

Hall

Utility

wc

Garage

GROUND FLOOR

FLOORPLAN

The double-aspect ground floor sitting room runs the full width of the house, and there is a separate dining room, kitchen, large utility, WC and cloakroom leading off from the entrance hall. Upstairs, the master bedroom has an en-suite bathroom, with a further bathroom shared by three additional bedrooms.

FACT FILE

Names: Sandra and Eric Dolby
Professions: Housing needs administrator and sign maker
Area: Rutland
House type: Four-bedroomed detached house
House size: 150m^2
Build route: Selves
Construction: Timber frame, brick cladding, concrete roof tiles
Warranty: Zurich
Finance: Private
Build time: June '99-July '00
Land cost: £37,000
Build cost: £40,000
Total cost: £77,000
House value: £275,000
Cost/m²: £267
72%
COST SAVING

Cost Breakdown:

Structural engineer	£300
Foundations and over site concrete to dpc level	£3,400
Timber and plywood for frame	£3,146
Bricks	£3,959
Bricklayers (labour)	£4,750
Timber doors, windows and glazing	£2,741
Floor joists	£514
Roof timbers	£1,700
Staircase timber	£524
Underfloor heating and chipboard flooring	£3,822
Plasterboard	£735
Insulation	£735
Electrical materials	£683
Roof tiles	£2,790
Plumber	£830
Condensing boiler & unvented water heater	£1,800
Plasterer	£400
Kitchen unit doors	£500
Sanitary ware	£2,300
Miscellaneous	£2,500
TOTAL	**£39,622**

USEFUL CONTACTS

Architect Norman Tomson: 01572 821140; **Underfloor heating** OSMA: 01392 444122; **Bricks and concrete roof tiles** Banbury Brick Ltd: 01623 660941; **CLS timber** Woodbridge Timber: 01394 385484; **Plasterboard** British Gypsum: 08705 456123; **Kitchen doors** B&Q: 0845 222 1000; **Insulation** Rockwool Ltd: 01656 862621; **Builders' merchant** PCP Harris: 01509 504666

Paint colours were an important element of the design, with the rendered walls of the cottage painted in a pale olive green from the Dulux Heritage Georgian range.

BUDGET BRILLIANCE

Ann Donovan has replaced a derelict 19th century cottage with a new two-bedroomed home over 94m² that, despite costing just £84,000 to build, refuses to compromise on quality either inside or out.

WORDS: DEBBIE JEFFERY PHOTOGRAPHY: NIGEL RIGDEN

AT THE TENDER age of 22, Ann Donovan purchased four condemned cottages in the Welsh village of Cefn-Coed, demolished them and built a bungalow on the site. Thirty-five years later and she has just completed her second self-build project there – a pretty, traditional-style cottage constructed next to her previous home for an impressively modest budget of £84,000. This new house replaces an old stone cottage, circa 1840, which was last occupied by a milliner but had been demolished when Ann originally bought the land. Local architect Paul Overton of Stephen George Architects designed the new property, which makes the most of its difficult site and incorporates some unusual modern details.

"The builder had wanted me to build the original bungalow in the centre of the plot, but I decided to put it close to the boundary wall at the bottom of the old cottage gardens instead, giving me room to build again in the future should I need to," says Ann. "When my second husband died I felt that I simply couldn't cope with such a large garden as well as working full time, and it worried me to see it getting untidy. I spoke to Paul Overton about the idea of building another house, and he applied for planning permission for a property in the garden."

Ann was concerned that the planners would not grant permission for a dwelling on the small, awkward piece of land, but the fact that a cottage had ➤

Solid oak floors are used in the sitting and dining rooms, while buff-coloured tiles are used everywhere else.

once stood on the site helped to convince her to try. She and Paul Overton designed the new 94m² house in a similar shape and layout to the old milliner's cottage with a lounge to one side of the entrance hall, a kitchen and dining room to the other and two bedrooms upstairs. "I first met Paul 12 years ago when we both worked for the same company, and we've been friends ever since," says Ann.

"He felt that it would be better to have two good-sized double bedrooms than to try and squeeze in three smaller rooms, and as I live alone it seemed like the sensible thing to do. A tiny box room is pretty useless as a bedroom if you can't even fit a wardrobe in it."

Ann wanted a cottage design but preferred to avoid artificial beams and low ceilings. The new house has rendered blockwork walls and a slate roof with pitched dormer-style windows set into the roof space. The ground floor extends forward beneath a lower, half-height roof, which slopes along almost the full width of the front elevation — breaking up the façade and creating an unusual canopy and glazed fanlight above the double entrance doors. There was no opposition to the planning

"IT HAS BEEN DESIGNED EXACTLY FOR MY NEEDS, WITH SOME MODERN TOUCHES WHICH MAKE IT TRULY UNIQUE."

application from the other villagers, and the plans were duly passed by the local authority.

"I used my savings to pay for the new house," says Ann, who remained living in her previous home throughout the build. "It was a difficult decision because the money had been set aside as my future pension, but I knew it would be repaid once I sold my old bungalow. I didn't want to use cheap-looking building materials, however, and the aim was to keep costs down without compromising on quality. The roof is natural slate but it came from Spain instead of Wales because Welsh slate was just too expensive. I was adamant that I didn't want PVCu, and the hardwood windows were made by a joiner in the village and then painted — which cost more but look so much nicer, as well as being better for the environment.

"Living right next door meant that I could keep my eye on the builders, which did prevent one or two mistakes," explains Ann, who chose most of the materials herself and spent every weekend shopping around for the best prices. "In the evenings when everyone had gone home I would go up and plan where everything would go, and one day I realised that one of the sitting room windows was missing. Luckily the mistake was easily corrected, but spotting it early on saved the builders a lot of time and trouble. Paul Overton acted as official project manager and we worked together to make sure that everything ran as smoothly as possible."

When it came to designing the interiors, Ann was in her element. "It ➤

Ann painted the traditional style kitchen in Farrow & Ball's 'French Grey' to match the dresser.

FLOUR

The double entrance doors mirror those of the church which stands on the other side of the lane.
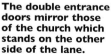

was a real luxury being able to choose things that I liked without having to compromise or consider what anybody else wanted," she says. "I'm particularly pleased with the kitchen, where the narrow dresser and small matching table were made by a company specifically to fit the space.

"I wanted a traditional kitchen rather than a sleek modern design, and managed to find an oak one in a local builders' merchant which I painted in Farrow & Ball's 'French Grey' to match the dresser. My grandmother used to have her kitchen table abutting the dresser door, so the layout is quite evocative for me and I bought a 1950s-style black refrigerator and a dual-fuel range cooker on the internet to complete the look."

Next to the kitchen, a separate dining room has been furnished with a table and four chairs, and a small desk means that it can also double as a study. Ann waxed the solid oak floors here and in the sitting room, which is reached through an angled door in the hallway and features a brick fireplace with a wood burning stove. The joiner who made the internal doors crafted a traditional oak mantle and a mirror for this room,

where a set of French doors lead out onto a flagstone patio.

Upstairs on the landing old traditional floorboards have been stained and varnished, and two large cupboards provide additional storage and house the central heating boiler. The bedrooms have sloping ceilings thanks to the dormer window design, and Ann can lie in her Victorian cast iron bed and look across at the church with its stained glass windows, which are particularly striking when lit from within.

"In the 70s it was common to replace old properties with new ones, but after we demolished the cottages I did wonder if we had done the right thing, despite the fact that they were beyond renovation," Ann admits. "Now I feel that I have given something back by building a house which is in keeping with the village. I called it Milliners Cottage in honour of the old lady who had lived in the original cottage, and bought some hatstands and old feathered hats as finishing touches, with a stone plaque set into the wall by the front door which reads 'Milliners Cottage 2004'.

"Everybody wondered why I was moving from the bungalow, but now that the new house is finished they can see that it has been designed exactly for my needs, with some modern touches which make it truly unique." ■

KEEPING TO BUDGET

Building a one-off house for under £100,000 is no small achievement, possible only by keeping down the size of the rooms, sticking rigidly to a fixed design and specification and running a tight ship. Ann Donovan has achieved all of this, bringing in her pretty 94m² cottage for just £84,000, yet still managing to create a home of great character and quality. The property is a fine example of how the best of old and new can be combined.

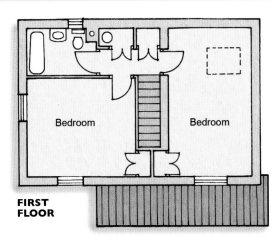

FIRST FLOOR

GROUND FLOOR

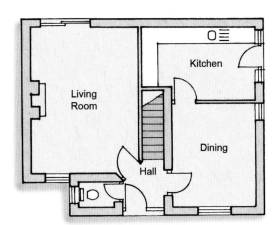

FLOORPLAN

The simple cottage plan has a sitting room to one side of the hallway and a kitchen and separate dining room to the other. There is a WC just inside the double entrance doors and a full bathroom upstairs which serves the two double bedrooms.

FACT FILE

Name: Ann Donovan
Profession: Training administrator (NHS)
Area: South Wales
House type: Two-bedroom cottage
House size: 94m²
Build route: Builder and DIY
Construction: Rendered blockwork, slate roof
Finance: Private
Build time: Sept '03-May '04
Land cost: £25,000
Build cost: £84,000
Total cost: £109,000
House value: £180,000
Cost/m²: £894

66%
COST SAVING

Cost Breakdown:

Preliminaries	£2,300
Demolition/alteration	£1,200
Excavation, earthworks	£2,395
Concrete work	£3,528
Brickwork, blockwork	£16,050
Roofing	£6,486
Carpentry and joinery	£20,094
Plumbing	£5,166
Drainage	£3,220
Heating installation	£4,900
Plasterwork and finishes	£6,247
Electrical installation	£4,258
Decoration	£1,410
External works	£3,633
Kitchen	£3,300
TOTAL	**£84,187**

USEFUL CONTACTS

Architect Stephen George Architects: 01685 371974 **Builder** Chris Jones: 01685 389509 **Joiner** Dave Rees: 01685 721277 **Builders merchant** Robert Price: 01685 383151 **Sanitaryware** Formula One: 01685 358600 **Slates** Cardiff Roofing: 02920 792122 **Timber flooring** ATC Monmouthshire Ltd: 01600 713036 **Internal doors** JB Kind: 01283 510210 **Antique lighting** Fritz Fryer: 01989 567416 **Farrow & Ball paints** Rabarts: 01685 379511 **Exterior paint** Dulux Heritage: 01753 550555 **Cast iron multi-fuel stove** Dovre Castings Ltd: 0870 780 4421 **Fabrics** Maskreys, Cardiff: 02920 229371 **Dresser and kitchen table** The Original Homes of Elegance: 01873 854906 **Range cooker** Rangemaster: 01926 457400

TRADITIONAL FARMHOUSE-STYLE HOME ✶ £150,000

The ground floor is based around an open plan farmhouse kitchen/dining room and living room. Richard and Anne have incorporated an oak beam to give the impression that the kitchen is actually an extension to the original barn.

TRADITIONAL VALUES

Richard and Anne Truesdale have built an attractive traditional farmhouse-style home for just £150,000 – and it is now valued at over £400,000.

WORDS: DEBBIE JEFFERY
PHOTOGRAPHY: CHRISTOPHER HILL

The exterior was inspired by the traditional stone farmsteads of the area which tend to have a farmhouse, barn and outbuildings arranged in a courtyard.

RICHARD AND ANNE Truesdale are a busy working couple with three children – Adam, 12, Victoria, eight, and Sophie, four – and a menagerie of animals who have somehow found the time to build two houses in the past seven years and are already planning their third. By adhering to a strict budget they hope that this final self-build project will leave them mortgage-free – enabling Richard, now 39, to take early retirement from his job as a photographer within the civil service.

"Richard and I both come from families who have built their own homes, so it just seemed natural for us to do the same," says Anne, 34. "Seven years ago we had the opportunity to buy a plot, and built slowly over three years, which allowed us to spread the cost. The house was a traditional cottage style home and we loved living there, but when a four acre rural site became available literally down the road, we decided to buy it. Our children have ponies, so we knew that the extra land would be very useful."

The couple approached the vendor and purchased the plot, made up of two fields, for £60,000. The site slopes from front to back, and outline planning permission had been granted for a one-and-a-half storey dwelling at the bottom of the hill. However, Richard and Anne immediately applied for full planning – relocating the site to the top of the

"WE WERE LUCKY ENOUGH TO HAVE A GREAT ARCHITECT AND TEAM OF BUILDERS WHO COMPLETED THE BUILD IN TEN MONTHS."

hill to gain light and views over the Mourne Mountains. They submitted their design for a two-storey rendered blockwork house with a barn-style wing attached by a brick link, and the planners agreed without any hesitation.

"We spent our weekends driving around the countryside studying old farmhouses. Sometimes we would ask the owners if we could take photographs, and they always took it as a compliment," says Richard. No part of the building is more than six metres wide, and the L-shaped house stands opposite a stable and garage block, creating an enclosed courtyard of what appear to be former farm buildings. "We wanted the entrance within the courtyard, and so what looks like the front porch is actually a bay window area in the dining hall, which gives additional floor space."

Inside, the Truesdales have used ideas which worked in their last house, ▶

Top-quality finishes include Chinese slate flooring over underfloor heating, granite and iroko worktops and maple units in the spacious kitchen.

Chinese slate, marble tops and wood panelling, plus a warm earthy colour on the walls, give the bathroom great charm.

including an open plan ground floor layout where the kitchen, dining and living rooms interconnect.

There is a separate adult lounge, a galleried dining hall for formal entertaining and a large utilities area which includes a cloakroom and shower room – ideal for when the children come in from the stables and need to clean off quickly.

Upstairs, the walls are continuations of the ground floor partitions, with each of the three children having identical-sized bedrooms and sharing a large family bathroom. "It saves any arguments," laughs Anne, who came up with the initial design herself and then employed an architect to redraw the plans and provide architect's certificates following site visits. "Our room is on the other side of the house from the children so that we can have some peace and quiet, and it has an en-suite bathroom and walk-in wardrobe. There is also a first-floor study area and a playroom, which doubles as a guest room. This may be accessed from an external flight of steps, which adds to the barn look and acts as a fire escape leading directly into the garden."

Initially, Anne and Richard had thought that they would need to sell their house and move into a caravan for the duration of the build in order to fund the project. After seeking advice they discovered that there was enough equity in their existing property to enable them to remortgage and continue living there, spending just two months on site in a caravan.

"We were lucky enough to have a great architect and team of builders who completed the build in ten months," says Richard. "Life in the caravan was an experience we wouldn't like to repeat, but it was only for a short time during the school summer holidays, which made it more bearable. We used to take caravanning holidays, but not any more!"

A budget of just £150,000 was set, which included building the five-bedroom house and the separate 198m² garage and stable block, with a tack room and self-contained mezzanine bunkhouse where the children can host sleepovers. In order to remain within this budget Anne kept strict records and took out accounts with several builders' merchants with which she haggled. Everything was meticulously planned, even down to positioning the furniture – placed on a floorplan in the form of paper cut-outs – which helped to dictate where switches and sockets would be located.

The Truesdales have no practical building experience and left most of ➤

"WE SPENT OUR WEEKENDS DRIVING AROUND THE COUNTRYSIDE STUDYING OLD FARMHOUSES. SOMETIMES WE WOULD ASK THE OWNERS IF WE COULD TAKE PHOTOGRAPHS, AND THEY ALWAYS TOOK IT AS A COMPLIMENT."

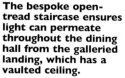

The bespoke open-tread staircase ensures light can permeate throughout the dining hall from the galleried landing, which has a vaulted ceiling.

the physical work to the professionals. They found that using a single building contractor to undertake the majority of the build was actually more economical than employing numerous separate subcontractors, and helped them to stay within budget. The final bill was just £250 more than the builder's initial quote, which covered some additional bathroom tiling.

Richard and Anne spent time visiting reclamation yards to purchase items such as Belfast sinks, the beams over the fireplaces and the sandstone hearth in the lounge, which was previously part of an old outbuilding. "We were drawn to salvage yards and managed to pick up some bargains – although prices do vary enormously from place to place," says Anne.

"We used granite heads and brick arches in the barn section to indicate where original openings would have been so that once the house was whitewashed in the traditional way the impression is of rendered stone. The structural arch over our living room fireplace is cut from Mourne granite and the uneven surface was worked by hand. With our family coming from Newcastle, in the foothills of the Mournes, no other granite would do. Even the 2003 date stone has Roman numerals so that, at first glance, the house cannot be recognised as being only a few months old!"

"Although we've only just finished building this house we are already planning our next self-build, using the same builder and subcontractors," Anne explains. "A smallholding and several acres of land have become available further along the road and, by building our third house, our mortgage will actually disappear. Building two houses and getting the third one free seems like an offer we can't ignore!" ■

FACT FILE

Names: Richard and Anne Truesdale
Professions: Civil servants
Area: County Down, Northern Ireland
House type: Five-bedroom house
House size: 280m², plus 198m² garage/stable block
Build route: Builder and subcontractors
Construction: Rendered cavity blockwork, brick link, roof tiles
Warranty: Architect's Certificate
Sap rating: 93
Finance: Bank of Scotland mortgage
Build time: Jan-Oct '03
Land cost: £60,000
Build cost: £150,000
Total cost: £210,000
House value: £400,000
Cost/m²: £314

48%
COST SAVING

Cost Breakdown:

Architect's fees	£3,000
Groundworks	£6,000
Builder – incl. blockwork, roofing, joinery etc	£81,250
Plumbing and sanitaryware	£12,000
Electrics	£5,000
Kitchen	£9,000
Stairs and external joinery	£4,000
PVC windows and door	£5,000
Fireplaces and wood burners	£1,500
Slate flooring	£2,000
Decoration	£1,500
Garage and stable block	£20,000
TOTAL	**£150,250**

FLOORPLAN

The ground floor has an open plan kitchen/dining area and informal living room, while a formal sitting room is separated from the rest of the house by a dining hall.

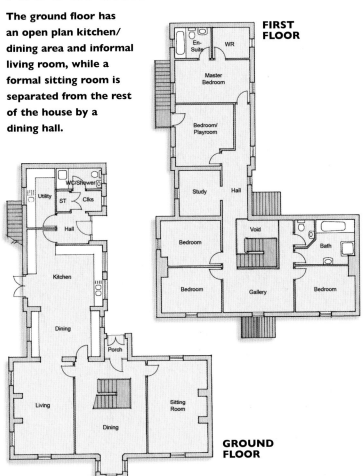

FIRST FLOOR

En-Suite / WR

Master Bedroom

Bedroom/Playroom

Study / Hall

Bedroom / Void / Bath

Bedroom / Gallery / Bedroom

Utility / ST / Clks / WC/Shower

Hall

Kitchen

Dining

Porch

Living / Dining / Sitting Room

GROUND FLOOR

THE PROPERTY LADDER

Richard and Anne mirror a significant number of people in that they view self-building as not only a means to create a unique home perfectly suited to their needs, but as a way to jump two or three rungs on the housing ladder at the same time. In Richard and Anne's case they have taken this to extremes by building three times with a view to paying off their mortgage. Richard and Anne's project was exceptional because of the relatively modest sums involved, the massive uplift in the value of their asset, the intricate attention to planning in order to ensure costs remained low, and, not least, the attractive result of a home that belies its low costs.

USEFUL CONTACTS

Designer – Crockard Building Design: 028 4483 1566; **Financial advice** – Compass Financial Services: 028 4483 1553; **Groundworks** – Bobby and Colin Paterson: 028 9756 3073; **Builder** – Aaron Clements: 028 4176 4995; **Plumber** – John Murdock: 078 6795 5274; **Electrician** – William Dodd: 028 9751 0321; **Granite** – I Hamilton & Sons Ltd: 028 4376 8206; **Wood burners** – Barns Style: 028 4176 4519; **Kitchen** – Natural Wood Kitchens: 078 0238 8549; **Windows** – T E Windows: 028 4176 3279; **Stairs and internal doors** – J C Joinery: 028 4481 1525; **Painter/decorator** – Stephen Strain: 028 4461 5319; **Wooden floors, beams and corbels** – Clarke Cunningham: 028 4482 8210

The aim when designing the new house was to include features similar to those found in barn conversions, such as a combination of brick and timber cladding, rooflights and a clay pantile roof.

LEARNING CURVE

Lynne and Stephen Wright's new
open plan timber-framed home has
been built on a modest budget

WORDS: DEBBIE JEFFERY
PHOTOGRAPHY: JASON BYE

A woodburning stove in the large brick fireplace provides a focal point for the open plan living room.

HEADTEACHERS LYNNE AND Stephen Wright are accustomed to creating order from chaos, but nothing could have prepared them for the sheer hard slog involved in managing their own self-build project. With such busy careers and four daughters to care for, the couple's dream of building a house had been put on the back-burner for a number of years, until they had enough time and the necessary funds to finally start looking for a plot.

"WE LEFT OUR COTTAGE BECAUSE IT HAD LOTS OF LITTLE ROOMS... THIS TIME WE WERE DETERMINED TO DESIGN A LAYOUT WHICH WOULD BE USED TO THE FULL"

"Stephen and I met while we were training to be teachers," says Lynne. "With four children to bring up on teachers' pay it wasn't easy, and we supplemented our income by renovating the houses we lived in – learning quite a lot about DIY along the way. We simply couldn't afford to pay for builders to do the work for us, so we bought inexpensive homes in good areas and did them up, juggling jobs, children and renovations. The last house we lived in before this was a 15th century cottage, and was all we could afford when we moved to Norfolk from Yorkshire. We added a large extension and designed the garden from scratch, which was very exciting at the time."

After completing this latest renovation project, and with their youngest daughter leaving home for university, the couple decided that the time was right to buy some land in the area and build their own house. They spent 18 months trying to find a single building plot before viewing an asbestos bungalow, which had been condemned as unfit for human

The open plan layout of the kitchen/dining/living room creates a spacious area suitable for large family gatherings.

habitation. Situated in a Conservation Area, the run-down property had formerly been used as a small holding and was hidden in overgrown fifth-of-an-acre grounds littered with sheds, outbuildings and greenhouses, with waist-high weeds and grass making it virtually impossible to walk up the driveway or even see the house.

"A rusty gate was held on with a bit of old washing line, but when we walked inside, it just felt right – as simple as that," Lynne recalls. "We loved that the site was already established, with mature trees making it very private, despite the fact that it's actually in a town centre location. Planning permission had already been granted for a boxy replacement brick bungalow, and what we considered to be a cheeky offer of £55,000 was accepted almost immediately."

Lynne and Stephen had already become avid readers of self-build books and magazines, and had previously visited the Potton show site at St Neots in Cambridgeshire, which gave them the opportunity to view

three timber-framed show homes in contrasting styles and to attend seminars where experienced self-builders spoke about their projects.

"We really liked the quality and flexibility of Potton's designs, particularly as we needed a house which would be suitable for between two and six people," Stephen explains. "To be honest, though, we didn't like any of their standard designs for the site. Our old cottage was a genuine oak-framed structure, so the idea of building a new house pretending to be old didn't really appeal. Although our daughters have left home they still visit regularly, and so four bedrooms and a spacious, open plan living area was vital. We wanted something more contemporary, without the beams and posts, so we based the design on Potton's Oakwell barn and then customised the layout to create a very light, sunny house. The entrance porch was extended and glazed, with our fourth bedroom positioned above this, and the kitchen, living and dining rooms have all been knocked together into one large space." ➤

"BUILDING OUR OWN HOME HAS BEEN EXTREMELY HARD WORK, BUT WE HAVE LEARNED A HUGE AMOUNT FROM IT AND MIGHT EVEN DO IT ALL AGAIN."

From the outside, the brick-and-timber-clad property resembles a traditional barn conversion, with a number of rooflights set into the clay pantile roof. Internally, the conservatory-style entrance porch leads into a hallway and the kitchen beyond, which is open plan to the dining and living room – forming an L-shaped area which features three sets of French windows and pivots around a simple brick inglenook-style fireplace. A separate utility room, WC, study, bedroom and en-suite bathroom make up the remainder of the ground floor plan, with three further bedrooms and a family bathroom upstairs.

"One of the reasons we left our cottage was that it had lots of little rooms which weren't very convenient," says Stephen. "We tended to live in one room while the rest stood empty, so this time we were determined to design a layout which would be used to the full. At first, the master bedroom was going to be on the ground floor, but problems with planning meant that the room turned out to be far smaller than we had anticipated, so we use this as a second sitting room instead. It faces west so when we get home from work it's full of sunshine.

"One of the most important things for us was that the house should be really bright," Stephen continues, "and the rooflights mean that the rooms are all filled with natural light. Upstairs on the landing we have a sofa, which makes this more than simply a space for passing through to reach the bedrooms. Our daughters argue over who will sleep where when they come to stay, and they love the room over the porch, with its sloping ceilings and conservation rooflights. Lynne and I have our bed positioned directly beneath the skylight in our room and can look up and out at the night sky."

The Wrights worked with Potton to design their new home and, once planning permission was granted, decided to manage the build themselves. As good organisers and keen DIY enthusiasts, the couple felt that they had the necessary skills to coordinate various subcontractors, and hoped to save money in the process.

"Although we were restricted to a tight budget, we didn't feel that we could go to work from a caravan," says Lynne, "so for 18 months we rented a house 15 minutes from the site. We have to dress professionally for our jobs and needed somewhere quiet where we

Birch-faced IKEA units and birch worktops were chosen for the kitchen, which is divided from the dining room by a free-standing unit.

could work at home as well, so a caravan on a building site would have been very stressful."

Stephen and Lynne both work in local schools and know many people in the area who were able to advise them on which tradesmen to use. Potton provided the entire timber frame kit, including windows and internal joinery, and were on hand throughout the project to offer advice. The main building contractor, C&K Beale, was able to recommend subcontractors. "During the summer holidays we were on site every day for six weeks, but it was difficult to fit everything in during term time," Lynne admits. "We had a lot of faith in the builders, however, which made our job far easier."

The couple were working to a tight budget of £150,000 and, although they did overspend slightly, they were able to save a great deal of money by undertaking all of the internal and external decoration, as well as laying the oak flooring, tackling the garden landscaping and buying inexpensive fixtures, such as the birch IKEA kitchen units which they built themselves.

"We had no water, electricity or flooring when we moved in," says Stephen, "but if we hadn't moved in then, we would have had to wait until the next school holiday. Building our own home has been hard work, but we have learned a huge amount from it and might even consider doing it all again when we need a smaller house for our retirement." ∎

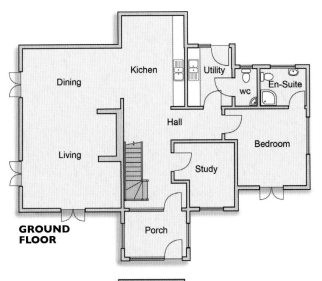

GROUND FLOOR

Rooms: Dining, Kichen, Utility, WC, En-Suite, Hall, Living, Study, Bedroom, Porch

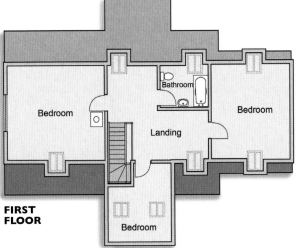

FIRST FLOOR

Rooms: Bedroom, Bathroom, Bedroom, Landing, Bedroom

USEFUL CONTACTS

Timber frame kit Potton Ltd: 01480 401401 **Stage payment mortgage** Norwich & Peterborough Building Society: 0845 300 2522 **Builder** C&K Beale: 01953 607486 **Carpenter/joiner** M Ling: 01953 860679 **Dry-liner** Lester Cooper: 01842 828648 **Scaffolders** Attleborough Scaffold Hire: 01953 453921 **Heritage Dark red multi bricks** Terca: 0161 873 7701 **Oak flooring** Petersons Natural Flooring: 01263 761329 **Hunter woodburner** Norfolk Stoves: 01603 860762 **Low-E glazing** Uniglaze (East Anglia) Ltd: 01603 741533 **Bathroom tiles** B&Q plc: 0845 222 1000 **Kitchen units** IKEA: 020 8208 5600 **Sanitaryware** Twyford Bathrooms: 01270 879777 **Taps** Bristan Ltd: 01827 304000 **Electrician** K Waterford: 01953 604109 **Sewer connection** MBW Contractors: 01953 453050 **Plumber** Graham Turner: 01953 453802

FACT FILE

Names: Lynne and Stephen Wright
Professions: Headteachers
Area: Norfolk
House type: Four-bedroom house
House size: 200m²
Build route: Potton kit and self-managed subcontractors
Finance: Private, and Norwich & Peterborough mortgage
Construction: Timber frame, brick and timber cladding, clay pantiles
Warranty: Zurich
Build time: Jan-Nov '03
Land cost: £55,000
Build cost: £167,000
Total cost: £222,000
Current value: £320,000
Cost/m²: £835

31% COST SAVING

Cost Breakdown:

Services	£3, 900
Demolition, asbestos removal and site clearance	£7,900
Frame and joinery (Potton)	£42,800
Electrics	£6,400
Carpenter	£7,700
Plumbing and heating	£6,300
Builder	£42,000
Landscaping, driveway	£7,400
Garage materials and erection	£13,000
Dry-lining	£6,300
Kitchen, sanitaryware, tiling, misc	£23,727
TOTAL	**£167,427**

FLOORPLAN

A glazed entrance porch leads into the spacious hallway, opening directly into the kitchen/dining/living room beyond. There is a separate utility room, WC, study and fourth bedroom with an en-suite on this level, and three additional bedrooms with a family bathroom upstairs.

BUILDING AN OAK-FRAMED DIY COTTAGE ★ £110,000

The Rosemary roof tiles were a costly requirement of the planners, but Ray managed to salvage enough from a local property to complete the main cottage as well as the adjoining garage for a fraction of the price.

HAND CRAFTED

Ray and Michele Blundell have created a dream oak-framed cottage built on a largely DIY basis.

WORDS: RACHEL JONES PHOTOGRAPHY: MARK WELSH

The beautiful oak floor is from Whitmore's in Leicestershire and was fitted by Ray using traditional brass screws under which he installed IPPEC underfloor heating. The fireplace was built using bricks from Terca.

WHEN RAY AND Michele Blundell decided to name their Staffordshire self-build 'Wild Thyme Cottage', their tongues may have been firmly placed in their cheeks, but their choice of name also summed up the journey of discovery that resulted in the creation of their dream timber-framed home.

A reclaimed butcher's block acts as the centrepiece of the traditional style free-standing kitchen.

As a keen long-distance runner, Ray, with Michele's support, is not easily deterred by a challenge. With a mixture of determination, hard work and just a little luck, the pair have become timber frame experts, deciding to tackle the majority of the build themselves, and while they are now enjoying the fruits of their labour, Ray in particular is itching to get his hands dirty again.

After two years of searching unsuccessfully for a suitable plot, in 1999 the couple were suddenly pitched in a frantic race against two other offers for a single building plot that Michele had spotted in the local free newspaper. ➤

"IT'S ALWAYS A COMPROMISE BETWEEN TIME AND MONEY WITH A SELF-BUILD PROJECT."

"WE WERE VERY CLEAR ON WHAT WE WANTED AND DEVELOPED THE PLANS TO REVEAL AS

MUCH TIMBER AS POSSIBLE WITH COSY PROPORTIONED ROOMS AND VAULTED CEILINGS."

"Time was of the essence and after so many months of frustration, we weren't prepared to lose out," recalls Ray. "Although offering the asking price, it was made clear that whoever could complete first would be successful, so in order to secure the deal, we took a gamble and made the decision to exchange before the results of the searches had been received – on the basis that the last application had been turned down simply because of the size of the proposed structure. When the news came through that the land was ours, we were over the moon – we'd beaten off the others by only two hours and it was also our anniversary and my birthday, so you can imagine the celebrations that night!"

But within days of their purchase, the couple were thrown into turmoil when a preservation order was placed on a number of trees on the site and they discovered that an impenetrable 130 metre layer of boulder clay ran beneath the plot. "The position of one tree in particular was causing us a real headache, but luckily it turned out to be diseased and we were granted permission to cut it down – creating the access we required for the site," explains Ray. However, the combination of thick clay and one of the wettest winters on record was to cause the couple more serious problems. "You'd

dig a hole and the next day it was full of water – nothing seemed to drain away, to the point where the whole site was a mud bath," says Ray.

A resubmission of the plans, taking into account the trees and the presence of clay, saw final approval granted for the project with trenchfill foundations stipulated at two metres deep onto which a block and beam floor was laid.

Following a visit to the Homebuilding & Renovating Show at the NEC, the couple had been impressed by the traditionally jointed and pegged green oak homes by TJ Crump. Taking advice from Crump's appointed architect, Ruth Read, they developed a design to their own specifications. "It was vital to us that the new build would project an established sense of character and atmosphere," says Ray. "We were very clear on what we wanted and developed the plans to reveal as much timber as possible with cosy proportioned rooms and vaulted ceilings."

Living at the time in rented accommodation, they decided to reduce their outgoings by moving into a static caravan on the site, which

A double-height atrium creates an impressive entrance to the cottage, made all the more spacious with the vaulted ceilings that were so crucial to the Blundell's design requirements, while a full-height window drenches the area with light. ➤

Initial quotes for the windows came in at around £16,000 but the Blundells managed to locate an excellent local craftsman, Peter Smith, who undertook the job for less than half the price.

also meant they were on hand to oversee the construction. Ray employed a local builder to construct a base course of bricks and shortly afterwards the timber frame, assembled at the Crump's Hereford workshops, was delivered to the site. Building was slow, not helped by the appaling wet weather. "The erection of the frame was incredibly exciting but took far longer than we expected, so I couldn't resist but to get stuck in myself," recalls Ray. "By Christmas, despite the site being a muddy bog, we'd managed to completely finish one gable end, and to celebrate we decked it with a holly wreath in an attempt to bring some festive cheer to the proceedings."

The final outer structure was completed in late January 2000, consisting of a green oak frame using six inch squared posts with rigid urethane

insulation infill panels sealed with weatherstrip, over which a lime render would finally be applied.

The planners insisted on the use of Rosemary clay tiles for the roof, and while driving over to his running club one weekend, Ray spotted a large old house tiled with Rosemarys which were in the process of being replaced. Ever the opportunist, Ray knocked on the door and asked the owner if he could buy the discarded tiles. They agreed on 15p each for 10,000 and he arranged for their removal. Reading up on the process, Ray and Michele decided to handle the entire build of the roof themselves and, apart from an unfortunate incident when Ray was blown off his feet trying to tie down a loose piece of felt (he cracked a few ribs

"ONCE WE'D BROKEN THROUGH THAT CONFIDENCE BARRIER WE FOUND THAT WE COULD ACHIEVE SO MUCH MORE THAN WE EVER IMAGINED POSSIBLE."

in the process) they managed to complete it successfully without any professional help.

"Safety obviously has to be paramount in these instances but it's always a compromise between time and money with a self-build project, so you have to make a decision on whether saving the money is worth the extra time and confidence required to handle a job yourself – in almost every case we decided it was," says Ray.

Turning their attentions to the internal features, the plastering was applied in a 'rough but satisfying style' and Michele set to work cleaning the beams with oxalic acid, after which they applied a hard-wearing water-repellent wax that they concocted in a pressure cooker in the caravan to their own recipe, giving the aged finish they were looking for.

Ray made all the internal battened and ledged doors using one inch oak boards with rosehead nails and chose oak floorboards and reclaimed limestone flags, under which they installed IPPEC underfloor heating powered by an Eco-Hometec condensing boiler with an unvented cylinder to provide direct hot water. Thanks to the timber frame's excellent insulating properties, the only other heat source is a woodburning stove in the sitting room. "As soon as the floor was down, Michele was out of that caravan like a shot," recalls Ray. "It was Christmas 2000 and the Christmas tree was in before I was!"

In September 2002, Ray started work on the next big project — an extension to the house in the form of a linked garage and office. Financing the construction with the VAT reclaimed from the original project, he built the entire structure himself to match the cottage. Using six-and-a-half tons of oak traditionally jointed and held together with pegs supplied by Crump and the remainder of the reclaimed Rosemary tiles on the roof, Ray utilised the skills he'd learned on the existing structure to superb effect.

Ray concludes, "We're both incredibly proud of what we've achieved with this project. We have a beautiful home that fits all the requirements we had when we first set our sights on a self-build. If we do another one, we'd certainly tackle the bulk of the work again ourselves. As runners say, 'When the going gets tough, the tough get going' and once we'd broken through that confidence barrier we found that we could achieve so much more than we ever imagined possible." ■

FACT FILE

Names: Ray and Michele Blundell
Professions: Sales director and self-employed child minder
Area: Staffordshire
House type: Traditional timber frame
House size: 210m² (including extension)
Build route: Self-managed
Finance: Barclays self-build mortgage
Construction: Traditional oak frame
Build time: Phase One: Nov '99-Jan '01; Phase Two: Sept '02-Sept '03

Land cost: £90,000
Build cost: £110,000
Total cost: £200,000
House value: £495,000
Cost/m²: £524

60%
COST SAVING

FLOORPLAN

The layout of the house revolves out from a central double-height dining hall/atrium space, with three bedrooms upstairs.

FIRST FLOOR

GROUND FLOOR

USEFUL CONTACTS

Timber frame company TJ Crump Oakwrights: 01432 353353; **Oak flooring and green oak timbers** Whitmore's Timber Co: 01455 209121; **Flagstone flooring** Hadley Reclaimed: 01283 575248; **Windows and staircase** Peter Smith: 07970 738305; **Bricks** Terca: 0161 873 7701; **Groundwork** Rene Harvey Groundwork: 07710 711765; **Bath** Calvari Rain Bath by Sottini: 01482 449513

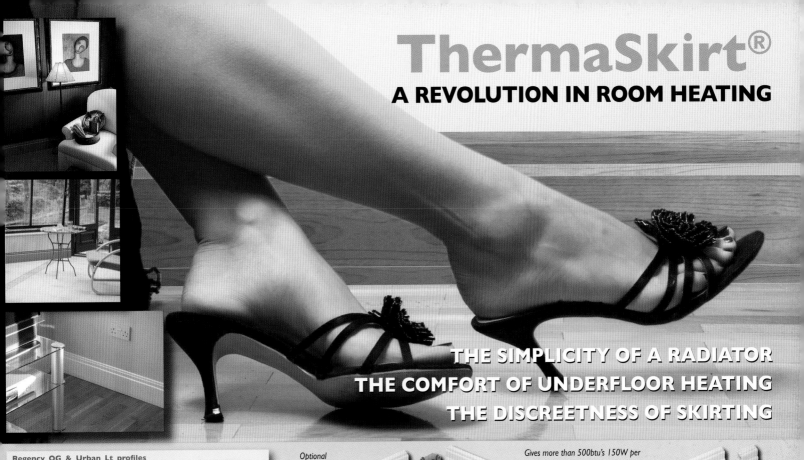
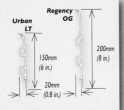

A PERFECT PARTNERSHIP

Building Your Own Home with
BUILDBASE

BUILDBASE HAVE DEVELOPED A SPECIALIST SERVICE TO PROVIDE THE SELFBUILD MARKET WITH A TOTAL MATERIALS SUPPLY SOLUTION FOR YOUR PROJECT.

Buildbase are committed to providing excellent customer service and we are confident we can supply all the materials you may need including any specialist or purpose made products.

Our huge buying potential ensures we always offer competitive pricing, which combined with experienced, knowledgeable staff means we can work with you to assist the successful construction of your new home.

FIRST CHOICE FOR ....

- CEMENT & AGGREGATES • BRICKS & BLOCKS
- TIMBER & ROOF TRUSSES • DRAINAGE
- DOORS & WINDOWS • PLASTER & PLASTERBOARDS
- PLUMBING & HEATING • TILES & FLOORING
- KITCHENS & BATHROOMS

FIRST FOR SERVICE ....

- PERSONAL CONTACT
- FREE DELIVERY & QUOTATIONS
- FREE ADVICE
- COMPETITIVE PRICES
- HUGE STOCK RANGE

BUILDBASE
A Great Deal More for the Builder

BRANCHES NATIONWID

Villavent® Comfort Conditioning™

The ability to 'choose' the level of comfort required within each individual home not just Heat Recovery but a lot more.

With the new Villavent Comfort Conditioning system, you can choose any combination of 5 key comfort factors to create exactly the right environment for your home.

Villavent Comfort Conditioning is healthier, delivering 100% filtered fresh air every day not just the recirculated air from a typical air-con system.

FIVE STAR TREATMENT AVAILABLE TO PICK AND CHOOSE FROM:

* Top up pre-heat
* Superb filtration
* Noise reduction
* Heat exchanger delivers warmed fresh air
* Comfort Cooling – Villacool™

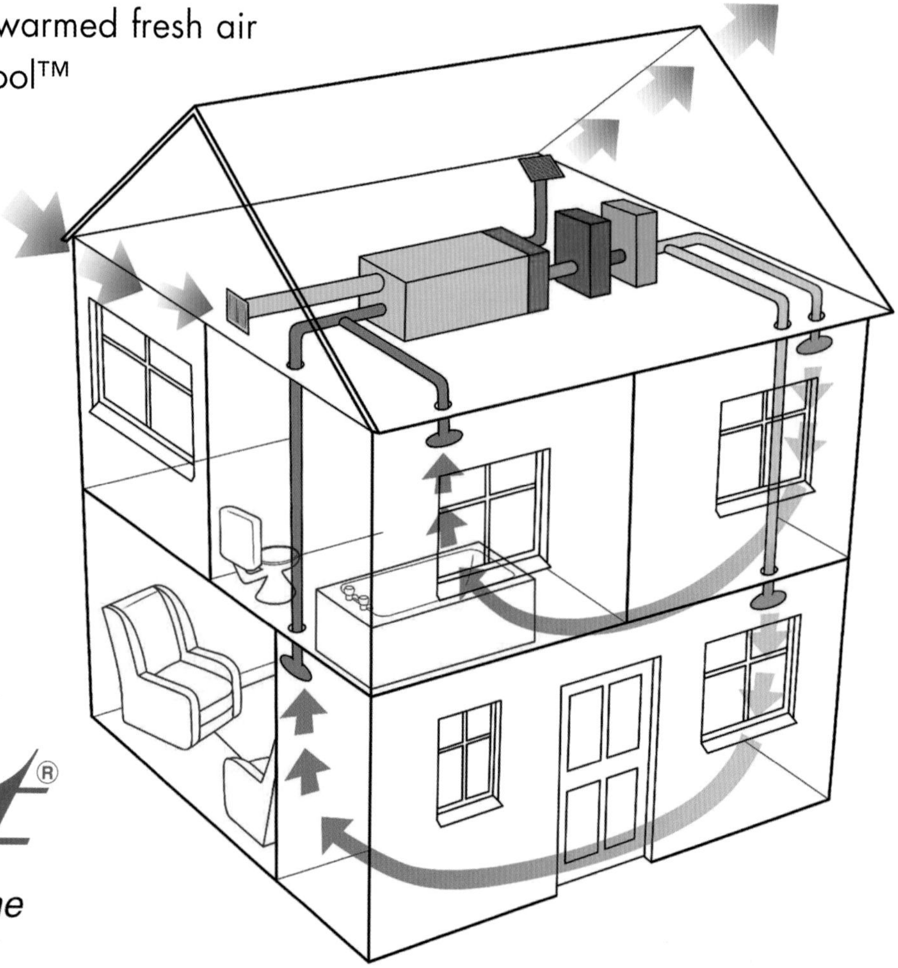

Villavent®

the ❤ of a healthy home

Villavent Ltd, Avenue 2, Station Lane Industrial Estate, Witney, Oxon OX28 4YL
T 01993 778481 **E** sales@villavent.co.uk **W** www.villavent.co.uk

Truly exceptional windows and doors. Only Marvin.

Marvin Windows and Doors are made for you. So they fit to your exact specifications, style, size and lifestyle. All handcrafted of beautiful wood, durable clad and a meticulous attention to every last detail. See the difference Marvin makes.

MARVIN®
Windows and Doors
Made for you.®

www.marvin.com

To see what Marvin can do for you, visit one of our showrooms or our website at www.marvin-architectural.com. Contact us by phone or e-mail today.

Marvin Architectural of UK	Marvin Architectural of Ireland	N. I: Window Crafters
Canal House, Catherine Wheel Road	Stephen Street	Omagh Enterprise Centre
Brentford, Middlesex TW8 8BD	Dunlavin, Co. Wicklow	Great Northern Road, Omagh BT78 5LU
Phone: 0208 5698222	Phone: 00353 45 401000	Phone: 028 8225 1300
E-mail: sales@marvinuk.com	E-mail: sales@marvin-architectural.com	E-mail: info@windowcrafters.co.uk

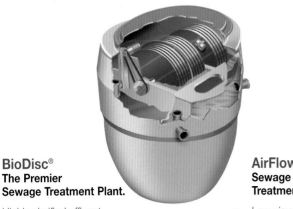

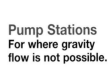
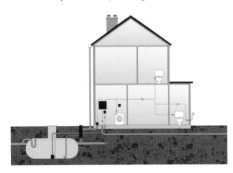

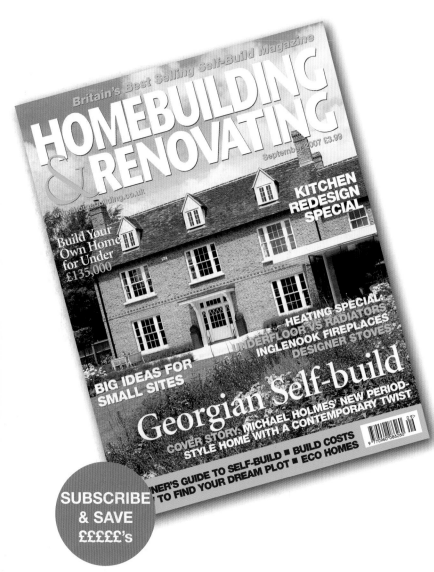